More of What You Thought You Knew about Judaism

More of What You Thought You Knew about Judaism

354 Common Misconceptions about Jewish Life

Reuven P. Bulka

JASON ARONSON INC.
Northvale, New Jersey
London

This book was set in 11 pt. Baskerville by Lind Graphics of Upper Saddle River, New Jersey, and printed by Haddon Craftsmen in Scranton, Pennsylvania.

Library of Congress Cataloging-in-Publication Data

Bulka, Reuven P.
   More of what you thought you knew about Judaism : 354 common
misconceptions about Jewish life / by Reuven P. Bulka.
      p.   cm.
   Includes bibliographical references and index.
   ISBN 1-56821-015-9
   1. Judaism—Customs and practices—Miscellanea.   2. Judaism—
Doctrines—Miscellanea.   I. Title.
BM700.B64   1993
296—dc20   92-44591

Manufactured in the United States of America. Jason Aronson Inc. offers books and cassettes. For information and catalog write to Jason Aronson Inc., 230 Livingston Street, Northvale, New Jersey 07647.

For
my dear wife
on our
25th anniversary

Contents

Acknowledgments

One of the most upsetting things that can happen to an author is to lose the only copy of a manuscript after it is well on its way to completion.

I know, because it happened to me. I was one-third of the way through the present volume when my computer crashed. Everything was one big, dark haze of nothing. All that work was down the computer drain. I had trusted technology with my only copy, and technology had let me down. Or maybe, since this was my first fling with the computer, I had let the computer down. We will never know.

The worst part of it all was that I could not see a time when I might ever build up the necessary psychic energy to reattempt the book from the very beginning.

But that is not where the story ends. When I related my frustration to a good friend and computer guru, he rushed to the scene and was able, through some wizardry that to this day I remember only as a dazzling blur, to rescue about 99 percent of the text, which was out of sequence and in disarray. But I had something to work with, and I resumed the book. Otherwise, it is doubtful this volume would ever have seen the light of day.

So, my first and most profound thanks go to the hero of the book, Hymie Reichstein.

As a continuing reminder of the mishap, the computer code for this book file was labeled "bkmess" (short for "book mess," which was as accurate a label as could be applied).

My dear parents came to visit with us over Pesah, and my father sacrificed quality time with his grandchildren and great-grandchildren to read the entire manuscript and offer valuable suggestions. This is just one more kindness in the vast expanse of my father's kindnesses, for which I am so grateful.

Blanche Osterer was, as usual, ever so helpful with various nuances of the manuscript. To her goes my ongoing appreciation.

It has been a real pleasure working with the people at Jason Aronson, including its erudite man in charge, Arthur Kurzweil. Arthur is a unique combination of scholar and *mentsch* — a delightful person to know and a treat to have as a publisher. My best way of thanking Arthur is to tell him that I hope, in a *kurz weil*, to have another book for you.

Appreciation is also expressed to Janet Warner at Jason Aronson for her patience, understanding, and effective editing.

Finally, this book is dedicated to the outstanding lady with whom I have spent twenty-five years of married life that have been, in retrospect, better than a dream. The reality of these years is far superior to any dream I may have had of what married life is all about. With a wife like Naomi, one can write books. Thanks for the lovely years and the editorial fine-tuning.

I hope this volume will be as favorably received as the first and will thereby prepare the path for a third volume.

Introduction

A number of years ago, when I first approached Arthur Kurzweil, now a cherished friend, with the idea of doing a book of misconceptions, he liked the idea and asked for a few samples. Dutifully, I sent the samples. He liked them but expressed skepticism about whether a book of misconceptions could be put together. Frankly, I shared that skepticism but did not let on. Instead, the skepticism became a challenge — truthfully, a challenge to prove Arthur wrong. And he was delighted.

The first volume contained 341 misconceptions. Why 341? I do not know, but after so many people asked me, I invented an answer. The numerical equivalent of the Hebrew word ASHaM (A — aleph = 1; SH — shin = 300; M — mem = 40) is 341. The word asham means trespass. And trespass often occurs because of misconception!

That was the first volume. Since then, based on the positive reception the first book received, I decided to try for a second volume. There is no more Kurzweilian skepticism. Nor should there be, because as I write this introduction to the now completed second volume, a third volume is already in progress.

This book contains 354 misconceptions. Why 354? The answer to the question is at the back of the book.

The misconceptions in this volume are less common than those in the first volume because they go beyond the basics. Based on recent findings about the level of Jewish knowledge, I suspect that what poses as a misconception may be simply not known. But I still consider them misconceptions because they do not seem logical at first glance. In addition, the somewhat informed will probably be surprised by many of the vignettes.

This is not to be taken as a legal volume. Though every caution has been enlisted to ensure accuracy, the main purpose of the book is to point out misconceptions. For legal decisions on the points raised, readers must consult their rabbis.

The citations attempt to be consistent, but this is not always possible because some of the books consulted as source material use various spellings. Readers who notice these discrepancies should therefore feel at ease about that.

Some sources list no year of publication, because no year is given in the actual volume. Sometimes, for the same reason, there is no mention of publisher.

Regarding the sources, the overwhelming majority are easily accessible. They come from the Torah, from the *Code of Jewish Law* (*Shulhan Arukh*), and from *Mishnah Berurah*. The sources are not exhaustive. They are intended mainly to give a head start to readers who desire to further explore matters.

In the introduction to the first volume, I expressed trepidation at the possibility of having left out a glaring misconception. I feel less trepidation with this volume, as I hope to issue a third, which will include the misconceptions that did not make their way into this one.

I welcome readers to share their own misconceptions with me, so that such can be shared with others.

1

Setting the Record Straight

Misconception: Adam was punished because he ate from the fruit that had been prohibited to him.

Adam's reaction, after being confronted with his breach of God's directive, was to tell God that the woman whom God had given to him as partner, Eve, was responsible because it was she who handed Adam the forbidden fruit.

Adam refused to accept responsibility for his action and actually implicitly blamed God. This he did through emphasizing that the woman "whom You gave to me" was the instigator.

Had Adam owned up to his responsibility, genuinely repenting his action, it is likely that God would have forgiven him. But he did not, and therefore God did not.

Misconception: The Bible states that humans cannot live beyond 120 years.

This is a misinterpretation of a biblical phrase, which states that a human being's days will be 120 years. It is not a statement that the human being can live only 120 years. The proof of this is that following this statement, the Bible goes on to report on many individuals who lived significantly beyond 120 years.

The biblical passage in question is really a reference to God's granting the human population at that time 120 years to come to its senses, to lift itself up from its moral abyss, if it desired to avoid the impending destruction.

Misconception: Noah took in two of each type of animal.

Noah took in two of each type of animal that was *tamay* (not eligible for human consumption). But of the type that were *tahor* (eligible for human consumption), he took in seven.

Misconception: The patriarchs were always wealthy.

When Yaakov fled his parental home to escape the wrath of his brother Esau, he left with hardly anything. What he did have was stolen from him on the way. When he arrived at the house of his uncle Lavan, he had nothing.

He left Lavan's house twenty years later with significant material wealth, gained from hard work. He would have been even better off had his uncle dealt honestly with him.

According to one view, Yaakov fled his parental home with hardly anything because his father, Yitzhak, had lost all his wealth.

Thus, at least two of the patriarchs were actually destitute, and for lengthy periods of time.

Misconception: Yaakov acted improperly in "forcing" his brother Esau to sell the birthright to him.

The sale of the birthright took place when Esau begged Yaakov for some pottage. Why was Yaakov making pottage? Children in their teens, as twins Yaakov and Esau were at that time, probably relied on their parents for their food.

Rabbinical commentary has it that the father, Yitzhak, was in mourning for the death of his father, Avraham. The children were now called upon to help with the needs of the house. Under normal circumstances, the primary responsibility for this fell on the shoulders of the firstborn, in this case Esau. But Esau was not to be found at home; he was in the field, enjoying himself. He came back tired and wanting to be fed.

Yaakov was understandably upset. He was saddled with a responsibility not primarily his. Esau, who should have taken care of things, showed no remorse. He only wanted to eat. Yaakov hedged on providing the food. He first wanted to set the record straight. Was Esau going to now take responsibility, or would he continue to be out of the picture? Yaakov asked Esau to sell him the birthright, to officially confirm that he no longer wanted the obligations of a firstborn. Esau did this, Yaakov fed him, and then Esau left without as much as a hint of remorse. He had effectively bid good riddance to the birthright mantle. Even after he had eaten, he did not bring up the subject, so as to perhaps renegotiate the deal.

Yaakov detected Esau's contempt for the birthright, even suffering the consequences of that contempt. If there was unfair behavior, it was on the part of Esau, who arrogantly wanted all the advantages of the firstborn but who thrust all its burdens onto his brother.

Misconception: Yaakov took from his brother Esau a blessing he did not deserve.

So it would seem from the biblical account. However, there is more to this than meets the eye.

Esau had long before contemptuously reneged on his birthright obligations. He sold his birthright, which at that time meant turning his back on all the responsibilities that rested on the shoulders of the firstborn.

The blessing bestowed by Yitzhak was a blessing to the family leader. It can hardly be argued that the family member who renounced that leadership should now be given that blessing.

Misconception: After marrying Leah, Yaakov worked another seven years before marrying Rahel.

After marrying Leah, Yaakov agreed to work seven more years in order to gain Rahel as a wife. But he married Rahel seven *days* after marrying Leah. He married Leah after actually working for seven years, but Rahel he married almost immediately after he had been deceived by his uncle and father-in-law, Lavan.

Misconception: As an act of revenge, Yosef delayed revealing himself to his brothers.

After Yosef had ascended to a powerful role in Egypt, his brothers came to Egypt for food. They came because Egypt, through Yosef's wisdom and leadership, was the only country in the immediate vicinity with abundant food during the famine. Yosef recognized his brothers, but they did not recognize him. This is not surprising, as the brothers hardly suspected that their brother, sold as a slave, would now be Pharaoh's chief viceroy.

Yosef did not reveal himself. Instead, through careful scheming, he engineered a scenario wherein the brothers were forced to react to the threat against their youngest sibling, Binyamin. It was only after they stood together in their steadfast resolve to protect Binyamin that Yosef revealed himself to his brothers.

Why did he wait till then? Because it was only then that Yosef was fully assured that the brothers had genuinely repented from their inexcusable behavior toward him. For Yosef to be reconciled, more than facile verbal contrition was needed. The brothers had to prove, to Yosef and to themselves, that they no longer were consumed with the pernicious envy that had precipitated their outrageous actions against Yosef.

Misconception: Yaakov asked God to introduce illness.

There is a rabbinic tradition that until Yaakov the patriarch, there was no illness. People died suddenly, via a sneeze. Not every sneeze resulted in death, but every death came via a sneeze. This, by the way, is behind the custom of saying "Bless you," or some other reactive blessing, when someone sneezes.

Based on the fact that it was reported to Yosef that his father, Yaakov, was ill, rabbinic tradition avers that this was a unique reality and one that Yaakov requested. Yaakov wanted people to feel a sense that life was ebbing so that they would take the time still available to set their houses in order and instruct their progeny. With a vital living will, children would be given crucial guidelines for how to live their lives.

But it is a misnomer, based on a faulty translation, to state that Yaakov asked for illness. Yaakov asked for what is called *hulsha*, which translates as "weakness." Rather than dying suddenly, he asked that people become weaker before they die. In this way, their posterity can become stronger.

Yaakov's was a prayerful wish for an ideal death process, a process that prepares both the departing and the surviving for what is to come.

12

Misconception: Were it not for the Egyptians, there would have been no Passover.

The fact that Israel was destined to go into slavery in a strange land had already been foretold to Avraham our patriarch long before the actual enslavement began.

Thus, it is eminently clear that Israel would have endured servitude, whether at the hands of Egypt or at the hands of some other enslaving power. And of course, part of that promise to Avraham was that following the subjugation, there would be a great deliverance.

Just as the enslavement was destined to occur, whether or not the Egyptians had been the enslaving country, so too the redemption and celebration subsequent to it would have been part of our history, whether via Egypt or via another country.

Undoubtedly, there would have been a Passover, a *passing over* from the state of slavery to the state of freedom. The intensity of the servitude might have been less severe under a different subjugating power than it was under the Egyptians. But the fact of slavery and redemption was already programmed to be a part of Israel's history.

Misconception: That we were enslaved in Egypt is an unfortunate part of our history we would have been better off avoiding.

It might seem absurd to think any other way but negatively about Israel's enslavement in Egypt. But there is more to this than meets the eye.

Distinction must be made between servitude and cruel subjugation. It is one thing to work hard and for long hours. It is another to be beaten, separated from wife and family, and have children either snatched away and killed or buried alive in the bricks and mortar in order to fill a work quota. The latter is more than unfortunate. It is despicable, inexcusable, and beyond rationalizing.

However, concerning enslavement, this fact of Israel's history had already been foretold by God to the patriarch Avraham long before the event. Why was it in God's plan that Israel go through a protracted period of enslavement before being redeemed and given the Torah?

One may speculate that it would be difficult for any group to fully appreciate the massive responsibilities that were to be thrust upon the Israelites. They were obliged to be sensitive to the orphan and the widow, to rigorously adhere to justice, to be sensitive to the plights and rights of others.

This is all nice in theory, but how does a group become emotionally tied to such ideals? Unfortunately, by living a life free of deprivation and full of material bounty, one is not likely to appreciate the poverty or deprivation of others.

But in being denied freedom and in having fundamental human expression trampled, one becomes both ever sensitive to the importance of freedom and of fundamental human expression and committed to fighting against those who would deny them. The Israelite experience of servitude was long and arduous but a necessary education in human sensitivity. By the time Israel accepted the Torah, it understood how important it is to be kind, to love the stranger, to protect the vulnerable.

This is *not* the reason Egypt subjugated the Israelites. But this is what we gleaned from the experience.

Israel's history of championing freedom and being in the forefront of bettering the world derives directly from the collective sensitivity it developed in Egypt.

Misconception: The Israelites became free when they left Egypt.

By the time the people of Israel left Egypt, they were free. They left as free people. They left in broad daylight, in open view, with heads held high.

They did not become free by leaving Egypt; they left Egypt as a free people. While in Egypt, they had already celebrated their freedom through sharing the Paschal lamb in a family setting and in open defiance of their subjugators.

Israel's freedom and dignity were not the result of a furtive escape and therefore contingent on circumstance. Israel's freedom is a fundamental reality over which no other people or nations have any ultimate power.

Misconception: The first commandments given to the Israelites were transmitted on Mount Sinai.

By the time the people of Israel arrived at Mount Sinai, they had already had a taste of Torah. At one of their stopovers on the way to Mount Sinai, at Marah, some regulations concerning *Shabbat*, honoring parents, and maintaining social order were transmitted to them.

That they were proscribed from materially creative endeavor on *Shabbat* undoubtedly reassured them that they would never revert to the type of protracted servitude they suffered through in Egypt. The honoring of parents was a basic staple of human interaction, as were the laws related to social order.

Thus, in three distinct dimensions—personal, interpersonal, and communal—they were given a clear sense of the responsibilities they were about to embrace. They gladly embraced this total package even before learning its contents. But God, in fairness to Israel, gave them a good idea of what was to come.

Misconception: The sixth commandment states, "You shall not kill."

The precise biblical words that constitute the sixth commandment are *lo tirtzah*. In some faulty translations, this is rendered as "You shall not kill."

This is a wrong translation. One in fact may kill if it is in self-defense or to protect a potential victim from a killer.

The sixth commandment translates accurately as "You shall not murder," meaning to kill someone in cold blood. This is the categorical prohibition we know as the sixth commandment.

Misconception: Yitro was always a non-Jew (non-Israelite).

At first, Yitro was not a member of the Israelite community. He is described in the Torah as being a priest of Midyan. But later on, when Yitro heard of the great deliverances wrought by God for the people of Israel, including the parting of the Reed Sea and the victory over Amalek after their surprise attack on the vulnerable young nation of newly freed people, he converted.

He became a believer in God and also became a member of the community of Israel, even though he did not continue traveling with the group.

It should be noted for the sake of accuracy that during Yitro's time, there were no Jews. The people who are now referred to as Jews were then known as Israelites.

Misconception: Jews were not capable craftspeople.

During Israel's sojourn in the desert, the people built a sanctuary to serve as a House of Service to God. This *mishkan*, and many of the artifacts contained therein, including the ark, with its cherubic figures, and the *menorah*, were all intricate structures.

Bezalel and his coworkers had to be outstanding artisans to have crafted these items. The *menorah*, for example, was made of gold and its intricate structure beaten out of one piece.

The *Bet HaMikdash* (Holy Sanctuary), built by King Solomon, was likewise a magnificent work, involving a large number of people.

Throughout the generations, Judaic artifacts designed to help in the fulfillment of religious obligations (*mitzvot*) were beautifully crafted. These include a wide array of items such as *Shabbat* and Hanukah candelabras, spice boxes for *Havdalah* (concluding blessings recited at the end of *Shabbat*), *etrog* (citron) boxes, *seder* plates, and charity boxes.

Jews were indeed capable craftspeople, but what they crafted was usually dedicated to religious use and therefore did not gain prominence in the outside world.

Misconception: Yehoshua was chosen as Mosheh's successor because he was the most naturally capable.

In terms of natural capability, there were others within the community of Israel who ranked higher than Yehoshua. It was not natural talent that gained for Yehoshua the distinction of being chosen as the successor to Mosheh Rabbenu. Yehoshua succeeded Mosheh Rabbenu because he was the ultimate disciple. He never left Mosheh, always staying close to him, observing firsthand how Mosheh guided the people. Others were more talented, but none was more dedicated and devoted than Yehoshua.

Misconception: The term *am haaretz* has always carried pejorative connotations.

The term *am haaretz*, as used today, means "ignoramus." Its original biblical connotation was quite different.

The first time this term is used in the Torah, it refers to a princely, respected leader.

The words, taken literally, mean "nation of the land." The literal translation suggests one who was a landowner and therefore quite powerful, almost a nation unto oneself.

Eventually, the term took on a more negative tone. It became a reference to a landowner who knew nothing more than how to take care of the land and was a boor in all else.

In a sense, one can understand this change through reference to a common word with changing meaning. One can say of another one that he or she is a "smart person" and, depending on the tone of the comment, it may mean either that the person is indeed smart or that the person is just the opposite.

Misconception: The *Code of Jewish Law* has always been universally accepted.

The *Code of Jewish Law*, commonly referred to as the *Shulhan Arukh* (literally, Prepared Table), is primarily the work of Rabbi Yosef Karo, a great sage of the 16th century who lived in Sefad.

His work, which codified the law, was at once hailed and attacked. It was hailed as a clear, concise, and authoritative guide to the fulfillment of Jewish law. It was attacked precisely because codification was seen by some as a dangerous stultification of the dynamic halakhic process. Others argued with some of the codified laws; still others questioned the right of Rabbi Karo to act as authority.

Another matter of contention was the feeling that the work did not take into account Ashkenazic custom and practice. However, to the great credit of Rabbi Mosheh Isserles, this problem was resolved when he appended to the work of Rabbi Karo the Ashkenazic view and practice when applicable. This greatly broadened the communal base of acceptance for the code, which paved the way for its becoming the primary legal guide for Jewish life.

Misconception: The *Code of Jewish Law* was the greatest work of its author.

Although the legal code written by the great sage Rabbi Yosef Karo had the most significant impact of all his works, the prolific rabbi produced other volumes of great importance.

One was called *Bet Yosef* (literally, House of Yosef) and was an extensive, brilliant commentary on *Arbaah Turim* (literally, Four Pillars), the work of Rabbi Yaakov ben Asher. The codes are gleaned from this commentary and are thus secondary to the primary commentary.

In addition, Rabbi Karo produced an extensive commentary on Maimonides' monumental work called *Mishneh Torah*. Rabbi Karo's commentary was called *Kesef Mishneh*. This latter work is considered Rabbi Karo's magnum opus.

Misconception: Many Jews chose the medical profession in the Middle Ages because of a natural penchant for healing.

Preoccupation with healing is ennobled in the Torah. For example, the *Kohanim* (plural of *Kohen*; descendant of Aharon and therefore charged with specific ritual responsibilities) were entrusted with custodianship of communal health. Also, the saving of life was accorded transcending value.

It is thus not surprising that many did have a penchant for healing, but the medical profession gained special prominence because Jews were often forbidden to engage in other occupations.

One option that remained open to them in that anti-Jewish climate was medicine. The study of medicine was often part of the course offering at talmudic academies, and many rabbis, including Maimonides and Sforno, became great doctors.

Medicine was one profession Jews could control in spite of the burdens imposed upon them. The hatemongers wanted neither Jews to cure them nor to cure Jews. Thus Jews were forced to take care of their own, and they did it well. In the process of such endeavors, they perfected many techniques and discovered medical cures that have greatly benefited all humankind.

Misconception: The Jews offered no resistance during the Holocaust.

After the Holocaust, this was at first the belief of many and the complaint of some, that the Jews marched like "sheep to the slaughter." But the verdict of history has gone through radical change with the passage of time and by way of survivors' testimony, both oral and written, about the courage and heroism of the Jewish people in the camps.

All this is aside from the well-known Warsaw Ghetto uprising. This uprising, as remarkable as it was, considering the oppressive circumstances, was not the exception. It was part of a widespread pattern of resistance.

In addition, it must be appreciated that those who did not physically resist resisted in a spiritual way. They maintained their dignity to the end, kept their faith at all times, and refused to compromise themselves just in order to live. For them, it was better to die and join God than to grovel in the Nazi hell. This represents resistance par excellence.

2

About This and That

Misconception: We are obligated to fear God.

The colloquial reference to our obligation to be God-fearing reinforces the idea that we are indeed obliged to fear God. But fear, wrath, and anger are negative components in any relationship. Surely our relationship with God should be of a positive, affirmative, loving, and embracing nature. It is very difficult to juxtapose love and appreciation with dread and fear.

The God-fearing colloquialism is rooted in an unfortunate error of translation. The Torah does ask us to *teer'a* God. Too many have wrongly translated this as the obligation to fear God. "Awe" is the more precise translation of the word *teer'a*. Thus, the more accurate and the more viable rendition of this directive is, "You shall be in awe of God." Awe is an inspiring attitude that engenders a positive, fulfilling, and embracing relationship.

Misconception: *Adoshem* is a proper way of referring to the Name of God.

There are many occasions when we refer to God either in the recitation of an excerpt of a passage not in the context of prayer or in the teaching of a lesson to children or adults. In such instances, we do not utter the Name of God. We merely make reference to God.

The Name of God as spelled out is *"a-do-noy."* There are many who have fallen into the wrong habit of substituting the word *Adoshem* when referring to God. This is a misnomer based on good intentions.

The Name of God is referred to as *HaShem*. *HaShem* means "the Name." We allude to God without mentioning the Name by referring to *the* Name, or *HaShem*.

Adoshem is neither here nor there. It is half of God's Name plus half of the reference to God's Name. But it is all of neither and should therefore never be employed.

Misconception: Some *mitzvot* are more important than others.

There are various consequences for noncompliance with certain *mitzvah* obligations. For example, the consequence for noncompliance with the *Shabbat* regulations is more severe than that for eating nonkosher food. Desecration of *Shabbat* is a capital offense, whereas eating nonkosher is not.

Some *mitzvot* may generally be more effective in transmitting a sense of commitment to Judaic affirmation. Others may be more important in specific situations.

But all this does not translate into a value judgment that ranks one *mitzvah* as more important than another. All the commands are God's instructions for life, and they are equally important.

Ranking the commandments is a dangerous exercise, with potentially harmful implications for the sanctity of observance.

Misconception: Judaic obligations are divided into the categories of positive and negative commandments.

The commandments of the Torah are divided into two categories—*mitzvot aseh* and *mitzvot lo taaseh*. These are the categories of (1) commandments one is obliged to fulfill and (2) commandments related to what one is prohibited from doing. They are usually translated as positive and negative commandments. This has become the standard translation of these phrases.

But even though these are the standard translations, they are incorrect. To suggest that there is such a thing as a negative commandment is erroneous and inappropriate phraseology. There are commandments one is obliged to fulfill and commandments regarding what one is prohibited from doing.

The more appropriate translation for these would be "affirmative commandments" and "prohibitive commandments." That which we are obliged to do, we affirm with our action. That from which we are enjoined, we are prohibited from doing. These are prohibitive commandments.

Misconception: The obligation to "love one's neighbor as oneself" is a general principle with no specific applications.

General though this principle may be, it is, like all other prescriptions, directed and tangibly expressed. The celebration of the joy of another person's marriage and the comforting of another individual who is in mourning are examples of sharing, which are specific fulfillments of the obligation to love one's neighbor as oneself.

Another component of this obligation is to avoid hurting other individuals by doing that which you would not want done to yourself. In its more affirmative sense, "love your neighbor" also entails the obligation to enhance the self-esteem of others by sharing positive feelings *about* the other *with* the other: complimenting, encouraging, and praising.

Misconception: Artwork composed of biblical verse is laudable.

The verses of the entire Scripture are sacred. They are the guiding principles and directives for living a meaningful, God-oriented life.

As much as artwork making use of biblical verses would seem to be a noble expression of Jewish cultural endeavor, nevertheless the sanctity of the biblical word as a holy guide is weakened in the process. It is reduced to an instrument of artful expression.

The motivation may be sincere and well meant, but the outgrowth of the motivation is highly problematic.

Misconception: The institution of animal sacrifice is barbaric.

The institution of sacrifice as spelled out in the Torah is anything but barbaric. The entire process was supervised by the *Kohanim*, the religious leaders of the community. All this unfolded in an atmosphere of sanctity and solemnity.

The actual process of sacrifice was akin to the kosher methodology of preparation of an animal for eating, with the same safeguards against inflicting even the slightest amount of unnecessary pain upon the animal.

In most instances, the edible parts of the animal were eaten. In a larger and more accurate sense, the sacrifices were actually the kosher preparation of an animal, with an additional religious dimension superimposed upon it.

Misconception: Sacrifices were intended to appease God.

Nothing could be further from the truth. God is not hungry or thirsty or set at ease by alleviating hunger or thirst, or overcome by anger and thus appeased by food or drink. Nor is God materially envious and likely to be calmed down with a present.

The main purpose of a sacrifice is to bring the individual closer to God. This is reflected in the biblical word for sacrifice, namely, *korban*. The word *korban* is related to the Hebrew word for coming close, namely *karov*. The purpose of the sacrifice was to bring the individual closer to God. Each sacrifice, especially if it were of the sin-offering type, also contained sincere verbal expression of repentance for whatever misdeed necessitated the bringing of the sacrifice.

God is undoubtedly angry when human beings behave in a wayward fashion and is pleased when human beings behave properly. But the anger is more a disappointment with the failure of human beings to do that which is proper and to actualize their spiritual potential.

When human beings behave properly, it is pleasing to God for the primary reason that the human being is thereby ennobled and closer to reaching the godly potential within. In the more profound and comprehensive sense, an individual coming closer to God pleases God, but surely not for what in human terms would be self-serving reasons.

God is pleased because such affirmation is most beneficial and meaningful to the human being.

Misconception: There is no problem associated with writing down words from the oral tradition.

The oral tradition—what we know of as the Talmud and its commentaries, a vast expanse of voluminous literature—was originally intended to be an oral tradition only. Had matters been left as intended, the Talmud would never have been written. We would have retained the vibrancy of an oral tradition transmitted from mouth to mouth through active learning and through energetic pursuit of knowledge.

However, the sages in their wisdom realized that if they maintained the oral tradition in its purely verbal form, ensuing generations would be denied this most valuable gift. This is because of forgetfulness, which would surely have compromised the accurate and complete transmission of that oral tradition.

Painfully but realistically, the sages realized that there was no choice but to reluctantly permit the writing down of the oral tradition—the Talmud and its commentaries.

In our generation, which has seen a veritable explosion of literature on the Talmud, both in Hebrew and in translated form, it is appropriate to realize that putting the oral word on paper is a necessary reality but not a desirable one.

Aside from the theological underpinnings, one may see in this a purely pedagogical rationale. When one studies from a book, one does not gain as accurate a comprehension of the intent and the nuance of the lesson as when one learns from a capable teacher. The teacher can transmit accurately, can explain and elaborate in greater detail, and can share implications and ramifications of the particular knowledge that is being transmitted. A book is cold and unresponsive.

Of course, this is contingent on the right teachers being available, in the proper number, and coupled with students who are attentive to the teachings. But it is always preferable to have the human touch rather than to study from inanimate paper. The fact that we have committed the tradition to writing is a lamentable reality of Jewish life.

It is important to keep this in mind, so that whenever one has the opportunity, one should run to study the authentic oral transmission from a capable teacher, relying on written text only when one has no other choice but to study from a book.

Misconception: Mourning for the destruction of the Holy Sanctuary (*Bet HaMikdash*) should come easily to a sensitive Jew.

The destruction of the Temple was a tragedy, the traumatic event that pushed Israel into exile and caused so many other traumatic events to occur, culminating in the Holocaust.

The mourning for the destruction of the Temple is in itself a complicated exercise, even for a sensitive Jew. It involves projecting oneself over history, back to a distant time, and imagining a reality that contemporary Jews have never experienced, namely, the full functioning of the *Bet HaMikdash*.

It is difficult even for a sensitive Jew to make this great leap backward and also project with such imagination. It is not an impossible task, but it is at the same time not an easy one.

It is important to realize this as one endeavors to appreciate the meaning of the *Bet HaMikdash* for Jews and for Jewish history. One who has difficulty mourning properly is not necessarily insensitive. It may be that one is actually trying hard, and that is most praiseworthy.

One should realize from the outset that the task is not easy and therefore one should not be deterred or depressed if unable to negotiate the distance and the time.

Misconception: Making predictions about when the Messiah will arrive is a harmless exercise.

It may seem as if prognosticating about the arrival of the Messiah is nothing more than a guessing game with no repercussions. However, history has shown the great danger of predicting the date of the Messiah's arrival. Whenever a date for the arrival of the Messiah was announced, and the people believed the announcement, when the prediction did not unfold, as was always the case, dire consequences resulted. The false Messiahs who made the predictions often induced their disciples to follow them onto wayward paths to cover up the false predictions. Such was the case with Shabbetai Zevi, among others.

The people who had put all their eggs into this redemption basket were often bitterly disappointed and sometimes just gave up on their faith.

Making predictions has always been a dangerous endeavor. The sages, in their wisdom, asserted that the bones of those who calculate the date of redemption should waste away.

Misconception: Being a *hasid* (disciple) of a *rebbe* (great rabbinic teacher) as one's ultimate religious relationship is an authentic Jewish practice.

The ultimate religious relationship is to be a disciple of God, to follow in God's ways, and to emulate God by being compassionate, kind, understanding, and responsive to the needs of others.

To the extent that the relationship with a *rebbe* inures toward that ultimate relationship, it is healthful.

To the extent that the relationship with a *rebbe* becomes an end in itself and is perceived to be the ultimate, it ceases to be Judaically authentic and in fact may become a distortion of fundamental Judaism.

Misconception: A *Kohen* who marries a divorcée may attend any funeral.

A *Kohen*, as a rule, may not marry a divorcée and likewise may not attend the funeral of anyone aside from the seven basic relatives (mother, father, sister, brother, wife, daughter, son).

Some people, including many who are *Kohanim,* think that if a *Kohen* marries a divorcée, he has thereby forfeited any connection to being a *Kohen* and is free to behave as if he were an ordinary Israelite.

This is not the case. True, a *Kohen* should not marry a divorcée. A *Kohen* who does so marry forfeits the advantages accruing to the *Kohen*. In modern times, the main advantage is to be the first called to the Torah.

But the obligations of the *Kohen* remain. The *Kohen* should not use one breach as an excuse to commit further breaches. The *Kohen* who is married to a divorcée should still not attend funerals aside from those permitted to any *Kohen*.

Misconception: Repentance makes one equal to a righteous person.

Repentance is a potent vehicle for redressing wrong and returning to God. Repentance contains the unique capacity to prevent the past from dictating the future in a negative way. One who repents from wrong is able to enter into the dialogue with God, unencumbered by past wrong. One is in fact forbidden from reminding the repentant person of previous wrongs.

Authentic repentance is a noble act worthy of great commendation. It is true that where repentant individuals stand, a righteous person cannot stand. But this may mean only that the righteous person may not be able to withstand a temptation that the repentant one has already tasted and can summarily reject because there is nothing enticing in it.

But the righteous person who has never tasted sin is definitely superior to a repentant person. Were this not the case, we would in fact be inviting individuals to sin in order that they could repent. This hardly makes sense.

Misconception: The concept of *Hillul HaShem* (desecration of God's Name) applies mainly to one's behavior among non-Jews.

There is certainly an obligation to behave in an upright fashion in all places, at all times, and among all individuals. It is our obligation to behave in the most noble tradition of the Torah no matter where we may be.

However, the major concept of *Hillul HaShem* is among Jews. It is here that the concept of sanctifying God's Name and avoiding the desecration of God's Name is most applicable. An individual who purports to abide by God's word, who then behaves in a totally unacceptable fashion, sets a bad example for others.

Those who witness the desecration will probably say that if this is what being godly means, they want nothing to do with it. They get the wrong idea of what God signifies. This is the ultimate desecration of God's Name, since it vilifies God and the godly message.

Misconception: The words "the *halakhah* says" constitute
proper phraseology.

Halakhah is Jewish law applied to life. Technically, the term refers to
the way that we should go, the way we should walk (*halokh*) in life.

Jewish law is not an independent construct, as if the law speaks
on its own. The law is a reflection of God's will as expressed in the
Torah and as expanded upon by the rabbinic sages over the years.
We abide by the *halakhah* not because the *halakhah* says but because
of what God says is the *halakhah*, the way to go, the proper way to
behave.

There is a danger that the focus on what "the *halakhah* says" may
deflect from the Original Source and from the more primary idea
that this is God's word that must be actualized.

To avoid this, it is better to say that the *halakhah is* rather than
the *halakhah says*. God says and the *halakhah* is.

Misconception: When a transplant from a deceased donor takes place, the unused parts may be thrown away.

It is the ultimate kindness for any individual to save the life of another. This kindness can be actualized in life and can also be achieved after death, via transplantation. The donor whose heart has given years to the life of a recipient has engaged in a most noble human expression.

However, the fact that one has saved the life of another does not therefore eliminate all the considerations concerning the dignity one must accord to the deceased.

There is no greater dignity for the deceased than that of gaining the credit for saving someone else. However, once that has been achieved, the unused parts of the donor's body, all of them, must be treated with as much respect as if they still were the entire person.

Therefore, all unused parts of the donor are considered sacred and must be buried together with the donor.

Misconception: Individuals who are more religious are more likely to be isolated from society at large.

The religious individual often spends time in serious meditation, whether it be via prayer or via study. But this endeavor is not an end in itself; it is, rather, a means. Through prayer, one becomes inspired by the godly imperative and is better able to confront life's ultimate goals.

Likewise, through meditation and study, one can become more aware of the responsibilities that confront an individual and be better able to exercise these responsibilities.

In fact, the more religious an individual is, that is to say, the more profoundly and authentically religious an individual is, the more likely that individual is to be part of society, concerned about society, and instrumental in helping society to gain its greatest potential.

As a general rule, one who is ostensibly pious but shows no interest in the well-being of the surrounding world is not authentically religious.

Misconception: The best preservative value in Judaism is to be set apart in a totally separated environment.

This is the argument that is advanced by some in order to justify isolating oneself from others not so religious. It is rooted in a fear that being involved with others may compromise one's own religiosity or the religiosity of one's offspring.

However, it is a wrong Judaism that is preserved through isolationism. Judaism is a life affirmation, which is predicated on concern for others, involvement with others, and the uplifting of others. This can hardly be achieved in isolation.

Isolation may increase the chances for survival, but it is the survival of a deficient religious expression and is therefore a dubious, ultimately self-defeating strategy.

Misconception: If one can afford it, there is nothing wrong with wearing expensive clothing.

It is obviously ill advised to buy expensive clothing when one cannot afford it. However, it is even improper to buy expensive clothing when one can afford it.

The reason for this is that wearing expensive clothing can lead to an individual's becoming arrogant and suffused with an exaggerated sense of self-importance that emanates from the "superior" dress.

At the same time, one should not go to the other extreme — that of wearing clothing that is cheap or tattered — if one can afford to wear decent clothing. In this and in so many areas of life, the best approach is that of moderation.

3

Tallit, Tefillin, Mezuzah, and *Kipah*

Misconception: The requirement to wash one's hands upon rising in the morning is rooted in superstition.

We often tend to brand as superstition practices whose logic is not immediately apparent. Such is the case with washing one's hands upon rising in the morning, which has been attributed to "evil spirits" that are on the hands.

The simple reason for the requirement to wash one's hands upon rising is the likelihood that during sleep, one may have inadvertently touched an unclean part of one's body. Thus, this requirement is a very sensible, understandable regulation that relates to Judaism's ongoing concern for health and cleanliness.

Another suggested reason is that upon awakening, we are as new beings, invigorated and ready to do God's work. This is symbolically reinforced through the washing of the hands, to sanctify them for God's work.

Misconception: One should cover the face when reciting the blessing for putting on the *tallit* (prayer shawl).

When reciting the blessing for putting on the *tallit*, we are instructed to wrap the *tallit* around the head in the manner that the Ishmaelites covered their faces. It is hardly likely that the Ishmaelites covered their faces such that they could not see in front of them.

It is therefore clear that when the *tallit* is donned, it should be placed over the face in a manner that still allows one to see what lies ahead.

Misconception: The top part of the *tallit* is the most important.

The top part of the *tallit* is certainly the most decorated area of the shawl. Some decorate the *tallit* quite lavishly, with fancy silver ornaments. This may give the impression that the top part of the garment is the most important part of the *tallit*. But such is not the case.

Were the top part of the *tallit* torn off, the *tallit* is still usable. But if a corner is torn off, the garment can not be worn as a *tallit*. Likewise, if the main body of the *tallit* is torn away, the garment is unfit for use as a *tallit*.

All this leads to the conclusion that there are other parts of the *tallit* that are more important than the top.

Misconception: When one removes one's *tallit* for whatever reason, one must recite the blessing when putting it on once again.

It all depends on the reason one removed the *tallit*. If, when removing the *tallit*, one had no intention of wearing it again for a while, and then one changed those intentions, then indeed one must recite a blessing when putting on the *tallit* again.

Surprisingly, however, if one goes to the washroom and removes the *tallit*, but with full intention of redonning it as soon as one returns, then one need not recite the blessing when putting it on again.

The reason for this is that technically, one is allowed to enter a washroom with the *tallit* on. It is only as an extra measure of respect for a *mitzvah*-fulfilling item such as the *tallit* that we do not wear it in the washroom. In this instance, its removal is temporary and nonradical. The intent to redon the *tallit* almost immediately precludes the necessity of reciting a blessing again.

Misconception: There is nothing wrong with wearing a *tallit* as a scarf.

It is obviously inappropriate to use a *tallit* as a scarf. This reduces a garment dedicated for religious expression to being a mere article of clothing.

The main point of concern revolves around the wearing of the *tallit*, during prayer, as a scarf. This too should not be done, because the *tallit* should ideally cover the greater part of the body.

One should be wrapped up in the *tallit* rather than having it hang around the neck.

Misconception: It is perfectly acceptable to wear a *tallit katan* (small shawl) by placing fringes on an undershirt.

In hot climates, this is quite a tempting option. However, it is not fitting that a garment designed to absorb sweat should serve as a *tallit*, small or large.

Therefore, as a general rule, it is preferable that the small *tallit* be worn over an undershirt.

Misconception: In order to pray, one must wear a *tallit*.

One should wear a *tallit* for the morning prayer. However, if no *tallit* is available and will not be available for that prayer, one should nevertheless proceed to pray without the *tallit*.

Misconception: Any natural string can be used as fringes for the *tallit*.

The string that is to serve as the fringe of the *tallit* must be made with the specific intent that it is for the purpose of being attached to the *tallit*.

Otherwise it is ordinary string with no fringe benefit.

Misconception: The *tallit* garment and its fringes can be of any color.

The *tallit* garment can technically be of any color, as long as the fringes (*tzitzit*) of the *tallit* are the same color as the garment to which they are attached. For example, if the four-cornered shawl onto which one is contemplating attaching fringes is a green garment, then the fringes should be green.

However, prevailing Ashkenazic custom is to have only white fringes. Since the garment and the fringes should match, it is therefore highly preferable that the garment also be mainly white.

Misconception: If a piece of the garment holding the fringes of the *tallit* tears, sewing the torn-off piece back onto the garment poses no problem.

If the piece in question is a significant part of the *tallit*, and its having become detached renders the *tallit* as temporarily unusable, then how the piece is reattached is not a simple matter.

If, for example, a corner rips off, then the *tallit* has only three corners with fringes attached. It is not a four-cornered garment and does not require fringes.

By sewing on the severed piece with the fringes on that piece to the other part of the garment with its fringes attached, one has assembled a *tallit* rather than having made it. Instead of the *tallit's* actually being made, it will have been created automatically by a sewing action.

When a significant piece of the *tallit* is severed, the fringes should be removed, after which the corner can be resewn onto the garment. Once that is done, the fringes are reattached to the resewn *tallit*.

It is essential that the *tallit* be made by direct human intention rather than spontaneously evolving from a tangential action.

Misconception: One may walk in a cemetery with the fringes of the *tallit katan* hanging out.

We are obliged to always be sensitive to the feelings of others. These others include not only the living; even the dead must be treated with sensitivity.

We do not assume that the dead feel nothing. Quite the contrary: we look upon the dead as having passed into another mode of existence, but it is existence nonetheless. We dare not insult the dead or mock the dead. Even an unintended mocking is forbidden.

Performing a *mitzvah* in the presence of the dead is insensitive. In the talmudic parlance, it is referred to as a mocking of the poor. The person performing the *mitzvah* may not so intend it, but the *mitzvah* action shows insensitivity to the dead, who cannot perform the *mitzvah*.

Even walking in a cemetery with the fringes of the *tallit katan* hanging out is proscribed for this reason.

The law programs an unrelenting sensitivity to the deceased. Adherence to the law (*halakhah*) helps to fine-tune that sensitivity.

Misconception: If one has no *tefillin* (phylacteries), one should not pray.

If one has no *tefillin* and is in danger of missing the deadline for the recitation of the *Shema* faith affirmation (that deadline being no later than the first three hours of the day), one should pray even without *tefillin*.

If *tefillin* will be available before the deadline, it is better to wait, but failing that, one should not miss the opportunity for reciting the *Shema* in its proper time.

Following the prayer, the heretofore *tefillin*-less person should seek out someone who will be kind enough to lend the *tefillin*, for enough time to don them and again recite the *Shema* (faith affirmation), but this time with *tefillin* on.

Misconception: All people place the hand *tefillah* (singular for *tefillin*) on their left arm.

This is true of all people who are right-handed. But not all people are right-handed.

Generally, one uses the more dexterous hand, usually the right, to place the hand *tefillah* on the less dexterous hand, usually the left. But if the person putting on the *tefillin* is left-handed, then for that person the left hand is the "right" hand to use in order to place the hand *tefillah* on the right hand.

In short, the left-handed person puts *tefillin* on the right arm.

66

Misconception: The leather straps of the *tefillin* are interchangeable.

There are *retzuot* (leather straps) for binding the *tefillah* of the head, and there are *retzuot* for binding the *tefillah* of the hand. Sometimes, when the situation arises, it may be necessary to replace one of the straps, and one may want to take it from another pair of *tefillin* that are not being used.

In such an instance, one must exact care in how this replacement is done. A *retzuah* that was once used for the hand *tefillah* can be used to once again function for another hand *tefillah*. The same is true of a head *tefillah* strap being placed on another head *tefillah*.

However, interchangeability poses its problems. One may use the leather strap from a hand *tefillah* for the head *tefillah*, but one may not take a head *tefillah retzuah* and change it into a hand *tefillah retzuah*. The reason for this is that the head *tefillah* has greater sanctity than the hand *tefillah* because it has four compartments and also the letter *shin* on it.

As a general rule, we must rise in sanctity and never go down in sanctity. A strap for a hand *tefillah* rises in sanctity when it is employed for the head *tefillah*, but a strap previously employed for a head *tefillah* would now diminish in sanctity if employed for the hand *tefillah*. For this reason, such interchangeability is proscribed.

Misconception: It is mandatory that the *bayit* (*tefillin* encasement) containing the parchment be black.

Black is the proper color for the *tefillin* box containing the parchment scrolls.

However, according to most halakhic authorities, if the coloring wears off and the black is discolored, this does not render the said *tefillin* unfit.

Misconception: If the black coloration on the *retzuot* fades, it does not affect the *kashrut* (acceptability) of the *tefillin*.

It is basic to the *tefillin* obligation that its straps be black. If the color fades, and the straps appear to be more brown than black, that is a fundamental deficiency in the *tefillin* that must be corrected.

This can be done either by applying black coloring to the straps or by replacing the discolored straps with new ones.

Failing these corrective measures, such *tefillin* should not be used.

Misconception: It is improper to wear *tefillin* when reciting *Selihot*.

Selihot are the special prayers recited very early in the morning at certain times in the year, including the week before Rosh HaShanah and the week between Rosh HaShanah and Yom Kippur. These are times when penitence is the order of the day, and the *Selihot* (literally, pardons) are the penitential prayers for these occasions.

In many places, *Selihot* are recited very early, when it is still dark. This is the ideal. When *Selihot* begin then, it is too early to put on the *tefillin*.

However, in many other places, for legitimate reasons, the *Selihot* are recited just a few minutes earlier than the usual daily prayers. It is light outside, and certainly the time when *tefillin* may be put on has arrived.

But because *Selihot* have been mentally linked to the earlier time, most people recite the *Selihot* without *tefillin*, even though there is no reason they should not have the *tefillin* on their hand and head.

It is slightly odd, to say the least, that at the time when we seek pardon, we should squander the opportunity to fulfill a *mitzvah*— here the *mitzvah* of wearing the *tefillin* for a longer time.

In fact, if the *Selihot* begins in the daytime, it is improper not to put on the *tefillin*.

Misconception: One is obliged to kiss the *mezuzah* (parchment scroll containing the *Shema* and the undertaking to fulfill the commandments) when entering and leaving home.

It is more than appropriate to kiss, or in other ways positively acknowledge and contemplate upon, the *mezuzah* when entering and leaving the home.

However, the essential obligation is to place the *mezuzah* on the doorposts of the home and all appropriate rooms. Kissing or other natural shows of affection and contemplation on this or any other *mitzvah* object are all highly recommended.

But there is a pronounced difference between recommended and obligated.

Misconception: Insofar as *mezuzah* is concerned, all houses are alike no matter where they may be.

If one purchases or rents a house, one is obliged to place a *mezuzah* — the parchment scroll containing two biblical excerpts — on the doorposts of that home.

However, there is a major difference between houses outside Israel and houses in Israel. Outside Israel, since our entire existence is not of a permanent nature, the obligation to place a *mezuzah* on the doorpost of a house becomes operative only after one has established a permanence in that house, namely, after thirty days.

This is not the case in Israel, which is our home. There the permanence of the land itself extends to the instantaneous permanence of whatever house into which one moves. Therefore, in Israel one must place a *mezuzah* on the doorposts of the home immediately upon moving into that home.

The basis for the instantaneous obligation with regard to *mezuzah* in Israel is linked to the obligation to inhabit Israel and to establish physical permanence in the land of our spiritual permanence.

Misconception: There is nothing wrong with wearing a *mezuzah* as an amulet around the neck.

The *mezuzah* is placed on house doorposts. It is there as a reminder to those who enter and leave that they must abide by the faith commitment, both in the home and in the public domain.

The *mezuzah* is not a magical instrument. It is not a good luck charm. It is a sacred alarm clock and reminder of our responsibilities.

It also should not be reduced to a personal charm that hangs on one's person. It makes no more sense to make an amulet of a *mezuzah* hanging from the neck than it does to nail the *mezuzah* onto the forearm of the individual.

The *mezuzah* is, by biblical directive, to be placed on the doorpost of the house. This is where it belongs. Putting it anywhere else both dilutes the message of the *mezuzah* and distorts what the *mezuzah* is intended to be.

Misconception: When moving out of a house, one must always leave behind the *mezuzot* (plural of *mezuzah*).

The *mezuzot* must be left only if those moving in are themselves Jewish and will therefore be in need of the *mezuzot*.

Also, if one leaves a house that one intends to sell, but no buyer has yet been found, one may remove the *mezuzot*. The same is true of a rented abode. If no new occupant has as yet rented the premises, one should take the *mezuzot* upon vacating the premises.

Misconception: A Jewish family moving into a home previously occupied by another Jewish family legally owns the in-place *mezuzot*.

It is hardly fair that one who has expended significant money for *mezuzot* should be obliged to incur a loss by leaving the *mezuzot*. This is especially so when the one leaving the *mezuzot* is moving to an abode with no *mezuzot* and for which a new outlay of money for *mezuzot* will be necessary.

The rule regarding leaving the *mezuzot* is not one-sided and insensitive to this contingency. One is obliged to leave the *mezuzot* for the party moving in. But the party leaving the *mezuzot* may ask for full payment of the cost of these *mezuzot*.

Further, all this applies to the parchments but not to the holders. The new tenants or owners have no claim whatsoever on the casings for the *mezuzot*.

Misconception: One may not throw a worn-out *kipah* (head covering) into the garbage.

It is important to cover one's head with a head covering that is called a *kipah*. However, this *kipah* is nothing more than a head covering.

It does not have the sanctity of a religious item, such as a *tallit* or *tefillin*.

As such, a worn-out *kipah* may be disposed of in an ordinary fashion, including throwing it into the garbage.

Misconception: For a head covering, one may put one's hand on one's head.

When one becomes aware that it is necessary to cover the head (by the way, it is necessary at all times!), one reflexively places the hand on the head if there is no *kipah* readily available.

However, covering the head with another part of the body is not a covering. The covering must be something that is external to one's body.

In such circumstances, it is therefore preferable to cover the head with a clean handkerchief or a napkin or even a flat piece of paper.

4

Prayer

Misconception: It is forbidden to take pictures in a sanctuary.

The sanctuary—the *Bet Knesset*, the place where people gather to pray—is a sacred locale. Certain activities that are inconsistent with the sanctity of the *Bet Knesset* should not take place there.

Taking pictures is not one of those activities. In years gone by, there were those who disallowed taking pictures in the sanctuary during weddings and other events that were held in the sanctuary. The main argument to support the position was that pictures were not permitted in congressional or parliamentary buildings.

But such should never have been the basis for normative practice. If taking pictures on weekdays is not prohibited, why create new difficulties?

By the way, by now not only are pictures allowed to be taken in congressional and parliamentary buildings but there is also ongoing television coverage of the proceedings therein.

Misconception: The *mehitzah* (separating structure in the *Bet Knesset*) is designed to isolate women.

Many sanctuaries, of both past and present vintages, were designed with little concern for ensuring that the women in attendance feel a part of the prayer service.

This is unfortunate, because it is important that women feel themselves to be involved in prayer rather than long-distance onlookers.

The *mehitzah* underscores the idea that prayer is personal meditation, not a social experience. That being the case, the *mehitzah* can and therefore should be so constructed so as to both separate the men and women from one another and integrate the women into the congregational expression.

Misconception: Only talking is considered an interruption of prayer.

Talking is definitely an interruption of prayer, but the primary objection to talking is that it deflects from the attention one must give to the prayers. Thus, reading a newspaper in the middle of prayers is an unwelcome intrusion into the prayer experience, even if it is done without talking.

Also, the time-honored but dubious exercise of making facial and hand gestures to convey a message during prayer may prevent a talking-type of interruption but still entails a serious rupture in the necessary concentration on prayer.

Misconception: Since Torah study is so vital, it is permitted to study it in the midst of congregational prayers.

Much as the study of Torah is desired, there are times when Torah study is not appropriate. One such time is in the midst of praying. Praying demands total concentration and focus, as it requires conversation about and with God. One can hardly pray with "all one's heart" when one's mind is on study, even if it is study of Torah.

Misconception: Before morning prayers, there are no inter-personal social obligations.

There is a fascinating, though not well-known, obligation that pertains prior to reciting one's prayers in the morning. It is the obligation incumbent upon each individual to accept the commandment to love others as one loves oneself.

With no unity and true concern among the earth's inhabitants, it is hardly appropriate to ask for God's concern. We have no right to ask God to do that which we are capable of doing but are unwilling to do.

Prayer to God can never and should never take place in a vacuum created by human insensitivity. Thus, the primary act of prayer in the morning must be preceded by our genuine expression of love for all our fellows.

Misconception: The louder one prays, the better.

It is important to hear the words that one prays. Such auditory sensation is helpful toward achieving and enhancing concentration.

However, screaming the prayers in a fit of devotion is not an improvement on the auditory theme. First, such screaming is insensitive to others and disturbs their prayers. Second, screaming suggests that God is hard-of-hearing and can hear the prayer only if it is yelled out. Paradoxically, such apparent show of faith reveals lack of faith.

Misconception: There are no restrictions on how loud one may answer "Amen."

"Amen" is the classical response that one makes to another who has recited a blessing. This is the way one expresses agreement with the sentiments of the blessing, namely, gratefulness to God for whatever reason the blessing has been recited.

However, there is an interesting and instructive regulation with regard to the response. The one who is answering "amen" should not raise the voice higher than the one who has recited the original blessing. The reason for this is that the one reciting the blessing and the one responding are equal partners in the exalting of God. The person responding should not try to become the "majority partner" by raising the voice and thereby assuming a more important role in the partnership.

It is a shame that this rule is not so well-known, because observing it reflects the human sensitivity that is such an intrinsic part of Judaic spiritual expression.

Misconception: Shaking and swaying in prayer are essential.

Many shake and sway during prayer. But to get the inner motor revved up to sway and shake as a required prayer motion can often be a case of mistaking a means for an end.

On the one hand, many people sway or shake. They do so spontaneously, as a natural motion that derives from their concentration on prayer. Tell them later that they were shaking heavily during prayer, and they may seem surprised.

On the other hand, others stand motionless, but not emotionless, as they pray. They find that they concentrate better when standing still.

Concentration is the key. For those who concentrate better when shaking, shaking is preferred. For those who concentrate better when standing still, asking them to shake is a mistake.

Misconception: *Aleph* and *ayin* in the Hebrew alphabet are pronounced the same way.

Although many people ignore the difference, there is a distinction between the ways that the *aleph* and the *ayin* are pronounced.

The *aleph* is a regular *a* sound, but the *ayin* has an *ng* ending to it. The difference is subtle, but it is real. The distinction between the letters should be respected in order to express accurately the words that contain these letters.

It is of interest to note that originally, a *Kohen* who could not enunciate these letters properly, pronouncing one like the other, was not permitted to recite the special blessing of the *Kohen*. Today, since most people are (unfortunately) unaware of the distinction, there is no reason to disqualify the *Kohen*.

Misconception: *Het* and *khof* in the Hebrew alphabet are pronounced the same way.

Most people think that the *het* and the *khof* are pronounced the same way. But this is not the case. The *khof* has a stronger sound, as in the name "Yokheved" or the word *halakhah*.

However, the *het* is pronounced somewhat more weakly than the *khof* but slightly stronger than the letter *hay* or its English equivalent, the letter *h*.

Thus, it is *Hanukah* rather than *Chanukah*.

Misconception: One who feels an urge to run to the washroom in the middle of prayer should continue praying rather than interrupt.

It is important to ensure that one's internal excess is evacuated before one begins prayer. However, it can happen on occasion that even after taking all the precautions, the need to relieve oneself suddenly arises in the midst of prayer.

In such an instance, one may tend to repress the urge and complete the prayers. This is especially the case when one feels that one can hold out for another five or ten minutes and that the prayer will take only that long to complete.

However, if the evacuational urge is so strong that one would not be able to control it for approximately seventy-two minutes, then one is not in the proper state of internal order to pray.

The rule here is that one must interrupt the prayer, even if this means removing the *tallit* and the *tefillin* to relieve oneself, and only afterward resume the prayer. This is the case even if by so doing one will miss the very important fulfillments of praying with the congregation and of praying within the proper time limit.

The reason for the rule is that praying in such a state of internal ferment is considered an abomination and must be avoided. So much so is this the case that if indeed one pressed ahead by reciting the prayers in such a state, such prayers are invalid, and one must pray all over again.

This is an important rule, and it addresses itself to both of the most vital issues of prayer: the sanctity of prayer and the state of the human body as it addresses its spiritual needs. Body state and spiritual state are inextricably linked to each other.

Misconception: There is nothing that can be done if one forgets one of the standard prayers.

The standard prayers are the evening (*Maariv*), morning (*Shaharit*), and afternoon (*Minhah*) services.

Each of these prayers must be recited in its appropriate time period: *Maariv* at night, *Shaharit* in the morning, and *Minhah* in the afternoon.

One who mistakenly forgets to recite any of these prayers and who is already past the time period for that prayer may compensate by reciting another *Shemoneh Esray* (*Amidah* prayer of nineteen benedictions) in the next time period, immediately after having completed the regular *Amidah* for that time period. For example, one who has forgotten *Minhah* should recite an extra *Shemoneh Esray* at *Maariv*.

Misconception: Concerning forgotten prayer, the *Musaf* is the same as any other prayer.

Musaf, unlike the standard prayers, is particular to its day. The *Musaf* prayer is the additional prayer for *Shabbat*, the festivals, and *Rosh Hodesh* (Head of the Month).

It makes little sense to recite this prayer when the *Shabbat*, the festival, or the *Rosh Hodesh* has passed.

With regard to *Musaf*, if forgotten, and the day for recitation of *Musaf* is past, it is a forgotten issue.

Misconception: There is no time limit on the making up of forgotten prayer.

The allowance to make up for a prayer that was not recited in its proper time applies only to the next immediate time period.

One can make up the forgotten evening prayer in the morning, but not in the afternoon. Forgetting once is an excusable accident. Forgetting again is a compound accident, which ranks in the category of negligence.

Such negligence is discouraged through not making available the compensatory avenue of repeating the prayer.

Misconception: One must cover one's eyes when reciting the opening declaration of the *Shema*.

One must concentrate fully when reciting the first verse of the *Shema*, because that verse affirms the fundamental Judaic monotheistic credo.

Full concentration entails the blocking out of all external stimuli. Covering the eyes helps in this, and such is the prevailing custom — to cover the eyes with the right hand.

In instances when for whatever reason it is not possible to cover one's eyes, it is sufficient to close the eyes and thereby shut off external stimuli in order to concentrate fully.

Misconception: The fact that the congregation is reciting the *Shema* has no implications for those in attendance who have already prayed or who are behind.

The *Shema* is the most vital affirmation of faith. So vital is it that any opportunity to express this faith should not be squandered.

At the same time, when the congregation is at the point of reciting the *Shema*, no one in attendance should give the impression of not being part of this vital expression. Solidarity through shared faith is too important.

Therefore, even one who has already prayed previously or who is behind (but in a place where interjection of *Shema* is permissible) should join the congregation in reciting the first verse of the *Shema*.

Misconception: One may never interrupt the *Shema* to recite the *Kiddush Levanah* (sanctification prayer over the moon).

Kiddush Levanah may be recited only until the halfway point in the month: halfway into twenty-nine days, twelve hours, and 793 parts of 1080. This is calculated from the exact moment of the birth of the new month.

Surprisingly, if, after reciting the *Shema*, the time for being able to recite *Kiddush Levanah* has passed (an admittedly rare possibility), one may pause at an appropriate place within the *Shema* to recite the *Kiddush Levanah* blessing only and then resume the *Shema*.

Misconception: Congregations wait for the rabbi to complete the *Shema* out of respect for the rabbi.

Not really. It may be disrespectful not to wait for the rabbi, but the reason one waits for the rabbi has to do with another issue.

All are generally aware of the importance of the *Shema*, but not everyone is aware of how vital is the last paragraph of the *Shema*, which contains mention of the Exodus from Egypt.

There is a biblical obligation to mention this, but since not everyone is attuned to the requirement, the rabbi traditionally recites that last paragraph aloud, to inspire the congregation to give proper attention to it.

Misconception: The *Shema* has always been part of the *Kedushah* in the *Musaf Amidah* for *Shabbat* and Festivals.

When the *Musaf* (additional) *Amidah* (main prayer) is repeated for the benefit of the congregation, the *Kedushah* (sanctification declaration) contains the first verse of the *Shema*.

Such a verse does not fit into a declaration of God's holiness. It is a statement of our faith in God and is obviously out of its proper context. It was not an original component of the *Kedushah*.

During the sixth-century persecution in the Byzantine Empire, spies would attend the houses of prayer in the morning, when the *Shema* was normally recited. A Jew reciting the *Shema*, declaring faith in God, was in grave danger, because this was forbidden by the persecutors. The spies would leave after the early-morning *Shaharit* had been completed, content that they had achieved their mission of assuring that the *Shema* would not be recited.

But our ancestors refused to capitulate. The *Shema* affirmation was inserted in the *Musaf Kedushah*, after the spies had left and while the people were still at the height of prayer.

We may not be in danger as were our ancestors, but we retain the *Shema* in the *Kedushah*. It serves as a reminder of the perils confronted by our ancestors, their unbending faith, and their tenacity and surpassing wisdom.

Misconception: The term *minyan* always refers to the presence of ten people.

The term *minyan* literally means "the number" and refers to the number that is required for a specific occasion.

For public prayer, the minimum number is ten people. But the term *minyan* is used for other situations when the prescribed count is not necessarily ten. As an example, the *minyan* of people that are to be called to the Torah on a weekday is three; the *minyan* of people to be called to the Torah on *Rosh Hodesh* is four; and the *minyan* of people to be called to the Torah for a Festival reading is five.

The minimum number of verses that must be read when only three people are called to the Torah is ten. This number ten is also referred to as a *minyan*; here, the number of verses.

Misconception: To establish a *minyan*, ten praying people are required.

It would be ideal if in the *minyan* of ten, all ten are part of the actual praying.

However, this is not a must. It is sufficient if a majority of the ten, namely six, are involved in the praying, with the other four just being present and responding to the blessings.

They may have already recited the prayer in question but can still form part of the *minyan*.

Misconception: To repeat the *Amidah*, one must always have a *minyan* of ten people present.

As a general rule, the Amidah is repeated by the cantor during the morning (*Shaharit*) and afternoon (*Minhah*) services, as well as during the additional service (*Musaf*) for *Shabbat* and the festivals.

The repetition of this prayer can begin only if the required minimum (ten) is present — what is termed a *minyan*.

However, if perchance one or more people leave the site of prayer, such that there are now fewer than ten people present at the services, the cantor, if he has already begun, may complete the entire *Amidah*, as long as the majority of a *minyan* (six) remains. He is not to stop in the middle or even if still near the beginning.

Misconception: For religious experiences requiring a *minyan*, having a large crowd is not that important.

There is something perceptibly majestic about a large crowd that gathers to celebrate an event. A large crowd generates an electricity that is inspiring and energizing.

This fact of crowd life is recognized as important in Jewish affirmation. When a minimum of ten for a quorum is required, the general rule is that the more who attend, the better.

The multitude reflect glory on God.

Misconception: The word *hazzan* has always referred to the cantor.

The cantor of the *Bet Knesset* is called *hazzan*. However, that title originally referred to an official of the *Bet Knesset*, one who assumed various duties in the functioning of the *Bet Knesset*.

Originally, the one who led the congregation in prayer was called the *shatz*, short form for *shaliah tzibbur* (agent of the multitude).

Over the years, with prayer services becoming more complex, it was natural that the *hazzan*, who was responsible for recitation of the proper liturgy, be considered the most capable to do this properly. Hence, the *hazzan* slowly but surely became the *shatz*.

Nowadays, even though many who serve as *shatz* lead only the prayer services, they are still referred to as *hazzan*.

Misconception: When the *Aron Kodesh* (Holy Ark) is open, anyone entering the sanctuary must stand still.

Some congregations, in the interest of decorum, either do not allow people to enter the sanctuary when the ark is open or urge them to stand in the back. Not being allowed in is itself a questionable practice, because it deprives individuals of a meaningful opportunity. Standing still in the back is likewise questionable. Those standing there are more likely to cause a disruption by their congregating in significant numbers. They are much better advised to go immediately to their place, to join the assembled in focusing on the *Aron Kodesh* and being part of whatever prayers are being recited at that moment.

Misconception: Prayer practices in Israel are the same as those outside Israel.

Generally, there is obvious and significant similarity between prayer practices in Israel and outside Israel. But there are also nuances of difference that distinguish Israeli practices from those of other countries. For instance, what would be the eighth day of Pesah, or Simhat Torah, outside Israel is an ordinary day in Israel. This is reflected in the prayer service.

Outside Israel, the general custom regarding the putting on of *tefillin* during *Hol HaMoed* (intermediate days of Pesah and Sukkot) varies; some individuals do, some do not. In Israel, the accepted practice is not to put on *tefillin* during these days.

In Israel, the lengthy prayer just prior to the evening *Amidah* (starting with the words *Barukh HaShem L'Olam*) is not recited.

There are other differences, including that the kohanic blessing is pronounced by the *Kohen* or *Kohanim* every day in some places in Israel; in other places in Israel, the blessing is pronounced every *Shabbat*. Outside Israel, this blessing is recited only on festivals.

These are just some of the variations in practices.

Misconception: The prayer for rain, recited in the daily prayers, is always recited at the same time in Israel and elsewhere.

In Israel, the prayer for rain commences two weeks after the conclusion of Sukkot (Tabernacle Festival), from the seventh day of the month of *Heshvan*.

Outside Israel, the convention is to start the request for rain about sixty days after the onset of fall, around December 4.

Israel commences its request for rain earlier, because it is higher than other lands and is in greater need of the rain.

5

Torah Matters

Misconception: The ancient Israelites' decision to accept the Torah without knowing its contents was a rash act.

Thus it may seem to outsiders, who have difficulty comprehending how a people could undertake to abide by an all-encompassing set of rules and regulations without knowing the actual content of those rules and regulations. However, this package was offered to them by God, who had just delivered them from protracted servitude.

That deliverance must have impressed the people with the feelings that God cared for them and was vitally interested in their welfare. God's set of rules for them could be nothing more than a continuing expression of divine concern.

In actuality, anything less than a full embrace of God's word would have been rash and irresponsible.

Misconception: Anyone may write a Torah scroll so long as the letters are written properly.

The words of the Torah are holy words, but a Torah scroll gains its sacredness from more than the words. For example, a photocopy of the Torah, though it must be treated respectfully, is not governed by the same set of rules as an actual Torah. The obligation to rescue a Torah, or to redeem it, would not apply to a photocopy of the Torah.

Likewise, a Torah written with scribelike precision but by a nonbeliever does not gain the status of a sacred scroll. If it were written by an artist who did not ascribe any sacredness to the Torah, that Torah would not attain the level of sacredness normally attributed to a Torah.

As with so many other elements of Judaism related to sacredness, this special status does not evolve automatically. It is attained through the sacredness that is attributed to the Torah scroll from the very outset.

Misconception: One who is in a state of being *tamay* (ritually distant) may not touch a Torah scroll.

The Torah is holy, sacred. But the sacredness of the Torah can never be compromised. Its sacredness is transcending, beyond human capacity to desacralize the Torah.

One who behaves inappropriately toward the Torah has not compromised the Torah but has surely compromised the self.

One who is *tamay*, be that person man or woman, cannot through being in that state transfer the *tamay* reality to the Torah. The Torah can never be so affected.

The *tamay* person who desires to kiss the Torah, to show affectionate respect to the Torah, may surely do so.

112

Misconception: The crown placed on top of the Torah is merely for decor.

The crown placed on the Torah certainly beautifies the Torah, in line with the general obligation to adorn the objects through which we serve God.

There is a second reason, however, for the crown's being placed on the Torah. The crown has bells, so that when the Torah moves, a distinct "Torah noise" is heard.

This serves as an alert to those in the vicinity of the Torah. It tells them that the Torah is passing and that they must therefore stand up out of respect.

Misconception: When there are *Kohanim* in the congregation, one of them must always be the first one called to the Torah.

The general operative principle of priority for being called to the Torah is that the *Kohen* is called first.

However, this is not always the case. In a place where everyone in the congregation is a *Kohen*, with the exception of one "ordinary" Israelite, that Israelite is called first.

The logic for this is that by calling the Israelite first, one avoids the possible conflict among the *Kohanim* as to which of them should be called first.

Peace is a powerful theme in Judaic affirmation.

Misconception: A *Kohen* who has married a divorcée may not be called to the Torah.

A *Kohen* may not marry a divorcée. Such action is a breach of the fundamental obligation pertinent to the *Kohen*.

In marrying a divorcée, the *Kohen* forfeits any of the advantages that derive from his status as *Kohen*. One of these advantages is the right to be called first to the reading of the Torah.

However, even though the *Kohen* cannot be called to the Torah as a *Kohen*, he is not worse than an ordinary person and may certainly be called to the Torah for those portions that are available to "commoners."

Misconception: It is obligatory to stand when the Ten Commandments are read in public.

It is the custom in many congregations to stand for the recitation of the Ten Commandments. This occurs three times each year—once each for the two times the Ten Commandments are spelled out in the Torah and once on Shavuot, the festival celebrating the giving of the Torah to Israel.

However, this is custom, not absolute law. In fact, some strong opposition has been voiced regarding the custom, as it suggests that certain parts of the Torah are more important than others.

Those who have always risen for the recitation of the Ten Commandments should not be surprised if they happen upon a community in which this is not done. Those who sit for the reading of the Ten Commandments are not derelict by doing so.

Misconception: That father and son, or two brothers, should not be called to the Torah one after another, has no logical explanation.

Some suggest that this caution is designed to ward off the "evil eye." But the primary logic for this caution is to avoid the charge that any family has a monopoly, or unfair advantage, in the protocols of the *Bet Knesset*. The principle of fairness is the main motive for this practice.

Because this is only a cautionary practice and not a legal breach, if a second brother, or a son, has been called and has gone up, he should carry through with the call to the Torah.

Misconception: Father and son can never follow each other in being called to the Torah.

It is general practice not to call a father and son, one after another, to the Torah.

However, if one of them is called for the last of the main readings and the recitation of the half-*kaddish* intervenes, then the other may be called for what is referred to as the *maftir* reading, if that reading is from a second Torah scroll, as is the case on a festival or special *Shabbat*.

Also, if the practice is not to call the *maftir* (the one who recites the *Haftarah*) by name, then in that case too, a son can follow a father and vice versa. A brother can follow his sibling as well.

Misconception: In being called to the Torah, one may take the same route to the *bimah* (center stage) and from the bimah.

When approaching the *bimah* upon being called to the Torah, one should take the shortest route. When returning to one's place, one should take the longest route.

This conveys the idea that we are eager to reach the Torah as quickly as possible and very reluctant to leave the Torah.

Misconception: One may lift up the Torah (*hagbahah*) at the conclusion of the reading without attention to the position of the Torah.

The right way to lift the Torah is with the Torah scroll open and showing three columns.

In addition, the seam where the parchment pieces are sewn together should be within these three columns. This allows for a more secure wrapping of the Torah.

One who is about to lift the Torah should first make sure the Torah is in such position, and if not, should roll the Torah to that position.

Misconception: The right way to lift the Torah is to stay in one place and move the Torah to the right and left.

The proper way to lift the Torah is to do so in such a manner that everyone in the congregation can see the three columns of the Torah.

The Torah is read on the stage, or *bimah*, which should be in the center of the sanctuary. There will be people seated in front of this *bimah* as well as at its sides and in the back.

If the person lifting the Torah moves only to the left and the right, not everyone will see the Torah script.

Therefore, the proper way to lift the Torah is to move with it, either in a full 360-degree circle or a full 180 degrees to the right and left, so that everyone properly sees the Torah.

Misconception: The prophetic reading following the Torah reading is called *Haftorah*.

Most people refer to the prophetic reading as Haftorah, as if the word relates to Torah in some way (*Haf-Torah*). But that is not the case. The word is linked to the idea of concluding, finishing. According to some, it is called thus because it is the finishing touch to the *Shaharit* (morning) service.

Therefore the proper pronunciation to project this meaning is *Haftarah*, as in "concluding."

Misconception: A mistake relative to the Torah reading has no bearing on the *Haftarah*.

The *Haftarah* is chosen from a prophetic reading that has a theme in common with the Torah reading most immediately preceding it.

When more than one Torah is used, the *Haftarah* relates to the last Torah reading. For example, on a *Shabbat* that is also *Rosh Hodesh*, the second Torah reading relates to the *Rosh Hodesh* theme. The *Haftarah* then relates to *Rosh Hodesh*.

There are times when three Torah scrolls are needed. It is then that mistakes in the reading order may occur. For example, on the *Shabbat* that is also *Rosh Hodesh* and *Shabbat HaHodesh* (the *Shabbat* when the *HaHodesh* portion is read, about two weeks before *Pesah*), three Torah scrolls are taken out of the *Aron Kodesh* (Holy Ark). The first Torah scroll is for the regular *Shabbat* reading. The second scroll is for *Rosh Hodesh*, since *Rosh Hodesh* comes more regularly (once a month) than does *Shabbat HaHodesh* (once a year). The third and last scroll is for the *Shabbat HaHodesh* reading. Since this is the last reading, the *Haftarah* relates to the *Shabbat HaHodesh* theme.

But what if a mistake is made, and the congregation recites the third reading second? In that case, the *Rosh Hodesh* reading, because of the error, becomes the third and last reading.

When that happens, the *Haftarah* also changes. One must recite the *Haftarah* for *Rosh Hodesh* rather than the *Haftarah* for *Shabbat HaHodesh*. This is the rule, because the *Haftarah* reading must relate to the theme of the reading immediately prior to its recitation.

6

Blessings

Misconception: The amount one must eat or drink to necessitate the initial blessing and the concluding blessing is the same.

In order to recite a concluding blessing, one must eat, at the minimum, a *kezayit*—food about the size of an olive. In order to recite a concluding blessing for liquid, one must drink at least a *revi'it*—a quarter of a *lug* (a little more than three fluid ounces).

However, one may not eat or drink even the slightest amount without reciting a blessing beforehand.

Obviously, then, the amounts necessitating blessing before and after eating or drinking are not the same.

Misconception: After washing, reciting the blessing, and eating a piece of bread, one need not recite blessings over any food during the meal.

The basic reason bread has an exemptive quality is that all other foods are subordinate to it. Because bread is the main staple, anything eaten with bread has been included in the blessing already recited for the bread.

But this applies only when the bread is the main staple. If one begins the meal with the blessing for bread, eats only a bit of bread, and then proceeds to an entire meal without eating any more bread, then obviously the bread is not the main staple.

Instead, the bread is being used as an excuse for not reciting other blessings. Clearly, this is unacceptable. When the other foods constitute the main meal, the blessings for them should be recited, and the bread should be avoided.

Misconception: The blessing recited over grape wine is always the same.

The usual blessing for grape wine is *Boray pri hagafen* ("Who has created the fruit of the vine").

However, should a second type of wine, say, of different sweetness or taste, be brought to the table, the blessing recited over it is *Hatov vehamaytiv* ("Who does good [for me] and makes good [for others]").

Misconception: The blessing recited for all types of wine is always the same.

If wine is derived from grapes, the blessing recited for it is *Boray pri hagafen*. However, this is not the prescribed blessing if the drink is blueberry wine, cherry wine, raspberry wine, and so on. For such wine, the blessing recited is *shehakol nehiyah bidevaro* ("that all was created by God's word").

If the drink is a mixture derived from grapes and other fruits, if the grape component is the majority, the blessing recited is *Boray pri hagafen*. Otherwise, the *shehakol* blessing is the appropriate *berakhah*.

Misconception: The concluding blessing after eating fruit is the same no matter where the fruit originated.

A special concluding blessing is recited after eating fruit. It is a condensed form of the first three blessings in the *Birkhat HaMazon* (After-Meal Thanks), recited following a full meal.

If a fruit originated in Israel, special mention is made of that fact in appropriate parts of the blessing. This represents a departure from the usual text of blessing. That departure, by the way, applies only to fruits through which Israel is exalted, including grapes, figs, and pomegranates.

Misconception: There is no special blessing that a guest bestows upon a host.

The Talmud records the specific text of blessing a guest should bestow on a host. This blessing is recited toward the end of the *Birkhat HaMazon*.

The approximate translation of the blessing is as follows:

> May it be God's will that this host not be shamed or humiliated, neither in this world nor in the world to come, and the host should be successful with all business dealings, that the dealings prosper and are conveniently close to the city. Let not evil forces have any power over the host's handiwork, nor should any semblance of sin or iniquitous thought attach itself to the host, from now and forever.

This is quite a nice blessing, more than just a general cliché no longer than a sentence. This blessing is of significant length and thought.

It is difficult to understand why this blessing was not found in the many standard prayer books or *Birkhat HaMazon* booklets.

Recently, the blessing has made a comeback. Some of the newer and more comprehensive *siddurim* (prayer books) contain it, and fancy posters presenting the blessing with attractive artwork have appeared on the market.

It is not a bad idea to carry this blessing along when invited to someone's house for a meal, if there is a likelihood that the host may not have the text available.

Misconception: At postwedding meals, the *Sheva Berakhot* (seven blessings) may be recited by seven different people aside from the one who leads the *Birkhat HaMazon*.

It is customary to honor individuals by asking them to recite blessings at postwedding meals. The meals themselves are referred to as *Sheva Berakhot*, a reference to the culminating blessings that come at the meal's conclusion.

These are recited during the seven days immediately following the wedding (the wedding day itself is the first of the seven days), when at least a *minyan* is present, one of whom is a new face who did not attend the wedding.

There are seven blessings that may be given out as honors. However, the last blessing, the blessing recited over wine, must be recited by the one who led the *Birkhat HaMazon*. This is the case when there is a *minyan* for any *Birkhat HaMazon* — that the one who leads recites the blessing for wine immediately following the After-Meal Thanks.

Thus, only the first six blessings can be given out to others, with the seventh already belonging to the one leading the *Birkhat HaMazon*.

Misconception: The text for *Birkhat HaMazon* in a house of mourning is no different from the ordinary.

The *Birkhat HaMazon* recited in a house of mourning contains special and poignant prayers for the comforting of the mourners.

Unfortunately, these prayers are not found in ordinary *siddur* texts, and the texts in which they are available are not readily accessible.

Some publications on mourning practices do contain these vital prayers. That they are not in most current, easily accessible *siddur* texts should not discourage the public from attempting to obtain this text for times when the need arises.

Misconception: The recitation of a blessing before and after a Torah reading has always been a basic component of Jewish practice.

Originally, only two blessings were recited at a public reading of the Torah. One was recited just prior to the beginning of the reading and the other following the conclusion of the reading.

However, because many people entered the *Bet Knesset* (House of Assembly for Prayer) in the middle of the reading or left in the middle, they may have assumed that no beginning blessing or concluding blessing is recited.

Such wrong assumptions were considered so serious that blessings before and after each reading were instituted. Each person called to the Torah now recites two blessings, unlike the original practice.

By the way, the importance of reciting a blessing both prior and subsequent to the Torah reading is to convey the idea that the Torah is not an ordinary book that one may casually read and put away.

The Torah is a sacred work and must be read in a sacred atmosphere, such atmosphere being engendered by the recitation of the blessings.

Misconception: A disliked *Kohen* should not recite the kohanic blessing.

Ideally, the *Kohen* is to evoke God's blessing for the congregation with "love." That is the mandate as incorporated in the *berakhah* recited by the *Kohen* just prior to reciting the blessing.

But a *Kohen* whose interpersonal behavior leaves much to be desired should still recite the blessing. We do not tell one who is deficient to add to that deficiency by refraining from other obligatory fulfillments.

As to how such a blessing can have any value, it should be noted that the *Kohen* merely recites. It is God Who bestows the blessing.

The *Kohen* who engenders a less-than-loving atmosphere is well advised to mend fences. That in itself is a blessing.

Misconception: During the time the *Kohanim* are reciting their blessing of the people, it is appropriate to recite certain verses.

Many *siddurim* contain verses that are to be recited by the congregation during the course of *Birkhat Kohanim* (the blessing recited by the *Kohanim*).

It is singularly inappropriate, even disrespectful, for the congregation to recite these verses when the *Kohanim* are reciting the blessing. It is wrong to do anything else but fully concentrate on and be attentive to their words of blessing.

These verses, if they are to be recited at all, should be said during the utterances of the *hazzan* (cantor), prior to the response of the *Kohanim*.

Many authorities recommend leaving out the verses altogether and focusing only on the words of blessing.

Misconception: It is universal practice that the kohanic blessing is recited only on festivals.

This is the practice outside Israel, but in most places in Israel, the kohanic blessing is recited daily.

Outside Israel, the pronouncement of this blessing is relegated to festivals because this blessing must be recited in an atmosphere of joy. During ordinary days, one is too preoccupied with the regular anxieties of life to be in a truly joyous frame of mind. Only on the festivals, with their mandatory immersion in the joyous festival ambience, are we receptive to this blessing.

In Israel, people also have anxieties. But the joy of being in Israel, at home, is so overwhelming that it justifies reciting the blessing daily.

Misconception: There is no special blessing recited upon recovering from illness.

Upon recovery from illness, one is obliged to express gratitude to God for the return to good health and to bless God, Who heals the sick (*Barukh Rofay Holim*).

This obligation is nothing less than logical and applies to illness of any type that causes one to be bedridden. We thank God for everything, including our health.

When the illness is more than a common cold, flu, or virus, and certainly when it involves surgery, the thanks that is expressed also includes *Birkhat HaGomel*, a blessing recited in a *minyan* of at least ten people. This blessing exalts God for having extended a largesse, here of health and vigor, to the one whose well-being was imperiled.

Misconception: *Kiddush Levanah* can take place indoors.

The sanctification service over the moon is akin to accepting the Divine Presence.

It is not fitting to do this indoors. One should go outside, the way one would go to greet royalty.

Only in extenuating circumstances, such as when one is ill and cannot go outdoors or when danger looms on the outside, should this sanctification be performed by the window or by the door, with the moon in view.

7

Kosher Tidbits

Misconception: Most consumers of kosher items in America are Jewish.

There are approximately six million Jews in America, and approximately six million consumers of kosher products.

Before you jump to the conclusion that these six million kosher consumers are Jewish, however, think again. Unfortunately, this is not the case. Only one-quarter of those six million are Jewish.

Astoundingly, the majority of kosher consumers in America are not Jewish; they are more likely to be Moslem. Moslems seek out kosher products because this fits in with their own dietary regulations, called halal. Seventh-Day Adventists, vegetarians, and health-oriented people are also part of this majority.

Not only are most kosher consumers not Jewish but it is also lamentably the case that most Jews are not kosher consumers.

Misconception: The rules of *kashrut* are primarily health regulations.

Eating what is kosher (fit) occupies center stage in Judaic affirmation. Adherence to the rules of *kashrut* requires a strong sense of disciplined commitment, both in the home and outside it.

There are those who have argued that *kashrut* laws are no longer relevant because we are so advanced in our knowledge of the effects of food on the body. The original *kashrut* laws were primarily health laws, goes the argument, and today we have better guidelines.

But this argument is faulty in many respects. Yes, there are health components to *kashrut*. God would not prescribe rules that are detrimental to health. But *kashrut* is more than awareness of health.

In health diets, one is permitted to cheat once in a while, but eating horse meat, for example, even once, is prohibited by Jewish law. *Kashrut* laws reflect a transcending concern for our physical and spiritual well-being. There is no compromise on this because it is not purely a matter of diet.

The higher moral principle associated with the proper preparation of meat, in a way that eliminates unnecessary harm to the animal, allows for no relaxation. Physically, there is no difference between an animal that was shot to death, then eaten, and one that was meticulously prepared, in a humane way, by an expert in that area, called a *shohet*.

But there is a great moral difference—a difference so significant that no amount of rationalization can excuse transgressing it.

The knowledge that we may eat only what has been prepared in a humane way represents one of the fundamental ideals of *kashrut*.

The rules of *kashrut* constitute more than health regulations. They are spiritually ennobling regulations.

Misconception: For food to be considered kosher, it must have a kosher insignia.

It is not the insignia that makes a food kosher. It is the fact that the food is kosher that facilitates the insignia.

Thus, certain items are kosher even without an insignia. Springwater, tomatoes, carrots, baking powder, plain flour, plain rice, sugar, wheat, and more need no insignia to be permitted.

Should there mistakenly be a kosher insignia on a can of pork and beans, the contents remain nonkosher.

Misconception: Washing hands after concluding a meal is not really necessary.

Generally, we are more aware of the requirement to wash hands prior to a meal than we are aware of the need to wash following one.

But it is wrong to dismiss the after-meal washing as unnecessary. After-meal washing cleanses the hands of any residual harmful salts or harmfully invasive foodstuffs that may have remained and that may, for example, through inadvertent eye-rubbing, cause severe problems.

Health and hygiene are too important to dismiss as trivial. We are obliged to sanctify ourselves through this kind of extra care.

Misconception: The requirement to maintain separate dishes for meat and dairy is biblically mandated.

Biblical law states that one may not seethe a kid in its mother's milk. This prohibition is stated three times, conveying not only that such type of cooking is forbidden but also that eating the mixture and deriving any benefit from it are likewise prohibited.

In other words, the Torah makes it quite clear that we may have nothing to do with such an admixture. But the parameters of what is biblically prohibited apply only to the mixture of meat and milk itself.

Rabbinic law greatly expanded the scope of the prohibition so as to prevent the possibility of meat and milk coming together. This includes having both separate preparative utensils and separate eating utensils for foods made of meat and foods made of milk.

In the end, separate dishes are part of the mandate, but it is always vital to know the precise source for the practice.

Misconception: The half-hour waiting period following the eating of dairy before the eating of meat suffices no matter what dairy product one has eaten.

Most dairy products available today do not remain stuck in the teeth, the way meat does. Also, meat, unlike cheese, gives forth fat and lingers longer.

Therefore, it is not surprising that few people are aware of the possibility that a six-hour wait may sometimes be necessary after eating cheese, before being permitted to eat meat.

This is the case with hard cheeses, cheeses so hard that they share common properties with meat. One seldom sees these cheeses on the market, but if such cheeses should be eaten, one would be obliged to wait the standard six hours before having meat.

Misconception: There is no rule against eating meat with coconut milk.

The milk that may not be taken with meat is regular milk, as from a cow. Coconut milk comes from a coconut and should thus be permissible with meat.

However, there is the danger that others who see someone having the combination may not be aware that the milk is from a coconut and may draw the wrong conclusion.

To prevent this from happening, it must be made clear to all that the milk in question is from coconuts. This may be achieved by having a coconut on the table during the meal or, better yet, by drinking the coconut milk from the coconut shell!

Misconception: Bread baked with milk is permitted to be eaten.

If the bread is kosher, and the milk is kosher, this should be the case, but it is not. Bread is a major staple that is usually a basic part of all meals, and one may accidentally use dairy bread in a meat meal. Therefore, to prevent such likely mishaps, the rule is to avoid dairy bread for use as daily bread.

Misconception: Ice cream is a solid food.

What difference does it make if ice cream is a solid food or a liquid food?

The rule is that in order to be obligated to recite a concluding blessing, one must have a prescribed amount of food—a *kezayit* (food the size of an olive)—in a prescribed amount of time. That amount of time is about nine minutes. If one ate the precise amount, but over a few hours, it is obvious this would not be considered real eating. It would be nibbling, and no concluding blessing would be necessary.

For liquids, the prescribed amount is a *revi'it*. Because it is normal to drink quite quickly, even nine minutes is too long. Thus, one who drinks in small sips need not recite a concluding blessing.

If ice cream is considered a solid, then eating a normal portion would necessitate a concluding blessing. But if it is considered a liquid that has been frozen, yet is still a liquid, then eating ice cream becomes the equivalent of drinking in small sips, and no concluding blessing would ever be necessary when consuming ice cream.

This is an intriguing dilemma, and the general conclusion is that for blessing purposes, ice cream is a liquid!

Misconception: Grasshoppers are a forbidden food.

Grasshoppers are not part of the Jewish diet, but that is not because grasshoppers are forbidden. Actually, by biblical law, grasshoppers, which, according to some, are referred to as *hagav* in the Torah, are permitted.

However, we are not exactly sure which grasshoppers are meant in the Torah. In order to avoid a potential biblical prohibition, we stay away from all grasshoppers.

Misconception: Human blood is a strictly forbidden substance.

As a natural reflex, we suck our finger if it has been cut. This may indeed help to stop the bleeding.

There is nothing wrong with this, and there is no requirement to spit out one's own blood after sucking it out.

It is the blood of others that is forbidden, not one's own.

Only if the blood has separated from its source and is found, for example, on a just-bitten piece of bread, should one not eat that blood. This is not because the said blood is forbidden. This is to avoid the prospect of others' seeing this blood and, not knowing its source, jumping to the wrong conclusion.

Misconception: For fish to be kosher, any scales are acceptable.

For fish to be kosher, they must have fins and scales. Fins and scales are the indications of permissibility.

All fish that have scales also have fins. But not all fish that have fins also have scales.

The scales that render the fish to be of the permissible variety must be such that they can be removed from the fish without removing the skin of the fish.

However, scales that are so closely attached to the fish that they cannot be removed without taking skin in the process do not qualify as scales. Fish with such scales are not permissible for eating; they are not kosher.

Misconception: The term *hallah* refers to a type of bread loaf.

In modern parlance, *hallah* usually refers to the loaf of bread that one purchases or bakes to grace the *Shabbat* or festival table, a wedding or *bar* or *bat mitzvah* meal, or other such festive occasion associated with a *mitzvah* fulfillment.

However, the biblical term *hallah* refers to something altogether different. It is a reference to the dough that is set aside from the entirety as a gift to the *Kohen*.

The only common denominator between the biblical term *hallah* and its modern usage is that both apply to dough. In the biblical understanding, it meant a part of it. In modern usage, it means the whole loaf.

Misconception: China dishes must be immersed in a *mikvah* (special body of water) before being used.

Generally, utensils used either to prepare food or to eat food must be immersed in a *mikvah* before being used. This immersion serves to sanctify the utensils for the purpose intended. That purpose is to sustain the body, through eating, in order to better serve God.

The immersion places the proper focus on the regular exercise of eating. But the requirement to immerse utensils applies primarily to metal utensils. Pure china is not metal and therefore need not be immersed.

Misconception: Only metal utensils must be immersed in a *mikvah* before being used.

The biblical regulation requiring that utensils for preparing or eating food must first be immersed in a *mikvah* applies to anything that is molten through fire. Metal utensils are the main types that fit this category.

Because glass can be prepared or repaired by being heated until molten, it resembles metal to some degree and was included by the rabbis in the requirement to immerse utensils.

Misconception: One may never destroy fruit-bearing trees.

The legislation that forbids the destruction of fruit-bearing trees is included in the biblical formulations regarding behavior during wartime. Even then, one may not destroy trees indiscriminately. But if the presence of the trees is life threatening in the war effort, one must destroy the trees in order to remove such danger to life.

There are other circumstances when destruction of trees is permissible, such as when the wood of a tree is worth more than the fruit it yields.

Misconception: When it comes to drinking, one must give to animals before humans.

One might reach this conclusion, based on the *halakhah*, that insofar as eating is concerned, one must feed one's animals before one feeds oneself.

However, insofar as drinking is concerned, humans come first. The reasoning is quite simple. Humans can more easily control the appetite than animals can. For animals, food deprivation may be quite painful, and we are obliged to be sensitive to this. Humans are accustomed to delaying their eating. They can wait, as they do on Yom Kippur and other occasions.

However, drinking is a more serious matter, because thirst may involve potential dehydration and its life-threatening implications. When it comes to preservation of life, humans come before animals.

Misconception: If there were no law against using harmful drugs, Judaism would also not prohibit such use.

Judaism's revulsion for drugs does not result from the fact that they are prohibited substances in society. Even were cocaine or heroin to be legalized, it would still be prohibited under Jewish law.

In Jewish law, any substance that is harmful to health is a forbidden substance. It makes no difference whether it is cigarettes, cigars, wood alcohol, cocaine, and so forth. Any substance with lethal potential is unkosher.

8

Shabbat

Misconception: Only women may kindle the *Shabbat* candles.

The primary obligation to kindle the *Shabbat* candles belongs to the woman of the home.

However, there may be either times when a woman cannot do so or situations when there is no woman to do so.

Within a family, there are times when the woman of the house is not home on *Shabbat*. It may be because of having to be out of town or because of childbirth or illness. Whatever the reason, it is then entirely appropriate, advisable, and required for a man to kindle the *Shabbat* candles.

In addition there are many homes without a woman in them but with bachelors, single-parent fathers, or widowers. All these should kindle the *Shabbat* candles.

Misconception: Having wine for *Shabbat Kiddush* is more important than having candles to kindle for *Shabbat*.

The *Shabbat* is ushered in with a sanctification called *Kiddush*, which is the verbal welcoming of the day and of its ambience into one's abode. The candles that are kindled on the *Shabbat* are intended to engender a spirit of optimism and luminousness in the home, literally to engender *shalom bayit*—the peacefulness and tranquillity of the home.

As important as it is to sanctify the *Shabbat*, the kindling of the *Shabbat* candles and the creation of a tranquil home atmosphere are even more vital. They go to the very heart of the primary thrust of *Shabbat* and of Jewish life in general, namely, to engender a tranquil atmosphere by fulfillments, which thereby brings about closeness between husband and wife and between parents and children.

Thus, those who are in the throes of poverty or other circumstances and who are forced into a painful choice between either buying wine or purchasing candles for *Shabbat* should opt for the candles. It is hoped that no one reaches this level of poverty. But if it does happen, then it is important to ensure that the environment of the house itself not be impoverished.

Misconception: *Shabbat Shalom* is essentially a greeting wishing others a good *Shabbat*.

Thus it would seem, judging by the intent of most people who extend this greeting. However, there is a more profound sense to the greeting. It is that "in the merit of *Shabbat*, you should be blessed with peace" (*shalom*). The first meaning conveys a friendly greeting. The second conveys a profound blessing.

Misconception: If one fasts on *Shabbat*, there are no lingering consequences for this breach.

Fasting on *Shabbat* is prohibited. The only time one fasts on *Shabbat* is when Yom Kippur occurs on *Shabbat*. Otherwise, *Shabbat* is a day of *oneg* (delight).

One may fast on *Shabbat* for various other reasons. It may be that one cannot eat on *Shabbat* because one may be where no food is available. That is obviously not a fast. Or a person may refrain from eating for medical reasons, which is again not a fast one desires.

One may decide to fast on *Shabbat* because one had a bad dream. This is usually standard procedure when having a bad dream. However, when a fast for a bad dream was on *Shabbat*, one must fast a second time in order to make up for the breach of having intentionally fasted on the *Shabbat* itself.

Misconception: If one lives within an area circumscribed by an *eruv* (*Shabbat* enclosure), one may carry anything on *Shabbat*.

The *eruv* enclosure effectively makes of the domain within it a private area in which carrying is permissible.

However, not all carrying is automatically permissible. Only carrying that is consistent with *Shabbat* would be permitted. For example, carrying a *tallit* to prayers would be permitted. Wheeling a carriage to prayers or for a *Shabbat* stroll would likewise be permissible.

However, transporting food from a house to another locale, for, say, a post-*Shabbat* meal, would not be permitted. Even though food may be used on *Shabbat*, this does not legitimize transporting food for use after *Shabbat*. This is forbidden even if one carries it within the *eruv* enclosure. The *eruv* enclosure removes only the carrying prohibition. Other *Shabbat* prohibitions attendant to the act itself are not nullified because of the presence of an *eruv*.

Misconception: It is permissible to carry a baby in a public domain on *Shabbat*.

There is a talmudic principle that a live person carries itself. This means that unlike the pure weight of a stone or other inanimate object, a live individual helps whoever is carrying that individual. A stone of twenty-five pounds weighs twenty-five pounds. A child of twenty-five pounds is slightly lighter because the child latches on and helps in the carrying.

However, it is wrong to jump from this to the conclusion that one may therefore carry a child in a public domain on *Shabbat*. The child does help in the carrying process, but it is still a carrying process.

The individual who carries the child cannot be considered culpable because the carrying is not an action carried out entirely by the carrier. The carried did help. However, carrying is a prohibited activity on the *Shabbat* and should be avoided.

It is primarily to help parents who desire to bring their children to the *Bet Knesset* for prayer on *Shabbat* that communities construct *eruv* enclosures where possible. This renders the area inside it as a private domain in which carrying is permissible.

Misconception: One who mistakenly lights a cigarette on *Shabbat* should extinguish it.

Obviously the kindling of a cigarette on *Shabbat* is a double offense. First, lighting and smoking a cigarette is wrong at any time; it is theologically prohibited because cigarettes cause disease and death. They are poison and therefore are prohibited by Jewish law.

Second, lighting on the *Shabbat* is itself a prohibited act. This refers to the lighting of anything, including lighting a cigarette.

The reflex reaction of someone who mistakenly lights a cigarette on *Shabbat* may be to put it out. Certainly the reflex reaction of someone who sees another lighting a cigarette on *Shabbat* may be to say to the person, "Put out the cigarette; it is *Shabbat*."

However, that reflex reaction, no matter how well intentioned, is not the right reaction. Not only is kindling a light on *Shabbat* prohibited but extinguishing a light on *Shabbat* is also prohibited.

Therefore, the proper reflex reaction to someone who has lit a cigarette on *Shabbat* is to tell the person to drop it. Of course, it is important to be sure that the drop takes place on a fireproof surface, so that it does not create the danger of causing a fire and imperiling life.

Misconception: It is perfectly acceptable to set one's television to a time clock and then watch television on *Shabbat*.

Too often, the focus on *Shabbat* is on what is prohibited. Certainly, there are many prohibitions associated with *Shabbat*. Part of the way that the experience of *Shabbat* is actualized is through the avoidance of these prohibitions.

But it is a mistake to think that merely by avoiding the prohibitions, one has fulfilled the *Shabbat* imperatives. The *Shabbat* is more than just the avoidance of prohibition. *Shabbat* affirmation entails the obligation to call *Shabbat* a delight and to remember the *Shabbat* in an active way through sanctifying it.

We sanctify *Shabbat* by making it a sacred day dedicated to study, to conjugal intimacy with one's spouse, to being involved in the welfare of one's posterity. These all are affirmative obligations, which are indigenous to *Shabbat* and fundamental affirmations of it.

The setting of a television to go on automatically on *Shabbat* and even having guards on the television to prevent the inadvertent changing of channels or raising or lowering of the volume may avoid the prohibitions that are associated with *Shabbat*, but they fail to address the affirmative obligation — to sanctify the *Shabbat*. We do not sanctify the *Shabbat* by watching television. In fact, we desecrate *Shabbat* through that.

Therefore, it is clear that watching television on *Shabbat*, however that television is spontaneously turned on, is a serious negation of the *Shabbat* ideal.

Misconception: There is no objection to looking up one's stocks on *Shabbat*.

Looking up one's stocks is a harmless exercise. It involves only shuffling pages and straining one's eyes to find the proper item and the figure attached to it. It certainly does not rank as creative labor and would seem to be a perfectly legitimate *Shabbat* exercise.

However, as harmless as it may seem, it is also a spiritually distracting activity. On *Shabbat*, our concern should be for the *Shabbat* fulfillments that beckon.

Shabbat is the time when we should suspend our weekday concerns about business, investment, and the turbulent world of the stock market. The focus should be on celebrating the *Shabbat* and allowing its spirit to pervade and guide our total activity on this spiritually uplifting day.

The focus should be on spiritual stock-taking, not stock-gazing.

Misconception: A person in the midst of *shivah* (seven-day period of intense mourning), if called to the Torah on *Shabbat*, should not go.

A person in the midst of *shivah* should not be called to the Torah, even on *Shabbat*. However, if called to the Torah, the refusal to heed the call would constitute a public display of mourning on *Shabbat*. Since such display is forbidden, one who has been called, even though in the midst of *shivah*, has no choice but to go.

Misconception: All activity generally prohibited on the *Shabbat* was prohibited in the *Bet HaMikdash*.

On the *Shabbat*, sacrificial offerings were brought in the *Bet HaMikdash*. Doing so involved actions that were otherwise prohibited, such as the ritual preparation of the animal.

This activity is explicitly mandated in the Torah and serves to establish a different frame of reference, in that some activities that are prohibited outside the *Bet HaMikdash* are permitted inside it.

One would normally think the reverse, that behavior in the *Bet HaMikdash* would demand greater stringency. The reason this is not so is that the sacred ambience of the sanctuary allows for expanded, *Shabbat*-oriented, and holy activity. Any fear that such activity may lead to the desecration of the *Shabbat* is quieted by the reality that the sanctuary offers a protective shield against such happenstance.

Misconception: Two blessings are recited prior to chanting the *Haftarah*.

They may seem to be two blessings, but they are actually one. This means that we should refrain from responding with the standard *amen* until the conclusion of the entire preamble to the *Haftarah*.

Misconception: The *Haftarah* has always been part of the *Shabbat* and festival services.

Originally, the scriptural reading on *Shabbat* or the festivals was from the Torah, the Five Books of Moses.

When the oppressors forbade the study or the reading of the Torah, the rabbis ingeniously ensured that the people remained aware of the biblical reading for each occasion by instituting the reading from a prophetic portion that shared a basic theme with the banned biblical reading.

Even though the original, perverse ban on biblical reading is thankfully only a memory, we retain the practice of the past, thereby gaining a better appreciation of the travails of our ancestors and perhaps some measure of gratitude because ours is a better lot.

Misconception: The *Havdalah* (the separation sanctification marking the conclusion of *Shabbat*) recited at the conclusion of the *Shabbat* is designed to separate the sacred from the profane.

The idea that the *Havdalah* separates the sacred from the profane is based on a faulty translation of the word *hol*.

We conclude the *Havdalah* with a blessing of God, who separates between *kodesh* (sacred) and *hol*.

But what is *hol*? The word *hol* does not mean profane, as if to suggest that outside *Shabbat*, everything we do is ugly and profane. Instead, the word *hol* refers to that which is ordinary—not non-sacred, but ordinary. The ordinary is important, even necessary, if we are ever to appreciate and value the sacred.

Misconception: The *Havdalah* ceremony signaling the end of *Shabbat* may be recited only on Saturday night.

The normal time for reciting the *Havdalah* is on Saturday night, as close to the conclusion of *Shabbat* as possible.

However, there are some occasions when, for whatever reason, one cannot recite the *Havdalah* on Saturday night. It could be that no appropriate drink was available. It could be that one was preoccupied with an emergency and unable to recite *Havdalah*. It could be that one was in the *onan* state — the period of mourning between death and burial — and therefore legally prohibited from reciting the *Havdalah*. Or, it could be that Tishah B'Av begins on Saturday night, and the *Havdalah* is not recited until after Tishah B'Av.

One may recite the *Havdalah* until Tuesday night because until Tuesday night, we are closer to the previous week than to the next week.

Misconception: A delayed *Havdalah* ceremony is exactly the same as *Havdalah* recited on Saturday night.

Not really. The *Havdalah* on Saturday night includes a cup of wine, spices with a fragrant smell, and a *Havdalah* candle of two or more wicks combined together.

The spices are part of the *Havdalah* ceremony because they tide us over the melancholy that comes with the exit of *Shabbat*. Because *Shabbat* gives us extra soul and extra invigoration, the passing of *Shabbat* makes us feel sad. We are perked up by the spices.

In addition, following *Shabbat*, we are once again permitted to make use of fire. This is symbolized by the blessing over the *Havdalah* candle.

However, these two ingredients are particularly connected to Saturday night. They are part of the *Havdalah*, but they are particular to a *Havdalah* recited on Saturday night.

By Sunday, the trauma of *Shabbat* ending has already passed and the permissibility of using fire has already been operative. It is therefore superfluous to employ these ingredients in the *Havdalah*.

The only ingredient that would remain would be the full cup of wine over which the *Havdalah* would be recited.

Misconception: One who has no candles or spices should not recite the *Havdalah* on Saturday night.

Although spices and a multiwicked candle are basic components of the *Havdalah* ceremonial, they are not imperative ingredients for *Havdalah*. In other words, if on Saturday night one has only a cup of wine available but no spices or candle, one should recite the *Havdalah* without these two ingredients.

The spices and multiwicked candle are appended to the *Havdalah* ceremonial because they are thematically related to the conclusion of *Shabbat*. But the ability to recite the *Havdalah* is not contingent on their presence or immediate availability.

Should the spices or candle or both become available later on Saturday night, the blessings over them should then be recited.

Misconception: One who has no appropriate drink over which to recite the *Havdalah* should not recite the blessings for the spices and the candle.

The *Havdalah*, as noted, involves a drink (preferably but not necessarily wine), spices, and a multiwicked candle.

When one cannot gain access to a cup of wine or other acceptable drink for Saturday night but does have spices and a candle, it would be correct to recite these blessings at that time, even though not in the context of the *Havdalah* ceremony itself.

Then, when the wine or other drink becomes available, the *Havdalah* should be recited in its entirety, aside from the already pronounced blessings for the spices and the candle.

9

Festivals and Special Days

Misconception: It is always ideal to usher in the *Yom Tov* (festival) early.

Generally, the idea of adding sanctity to the ordinary, by ushering in *Shabbat* or *Yom Tov* earlier, is highly recommended.

This may be done only after *Pelag HaMinhah* (approximately one and one-quarter twelfths of the day prior to sunset).

Even then, this may not be done for all festivals. Shavuot, which is fifty days after the second day of Pesah, follows the counting of the *Omer*, a forty-nine-day period.

Because these forty-nine days must be complete, the ushering in of Shavuot earlier would take away from the completeness of the forty-ninth day.

Therefore, the *Maariv* prayer ushering in Shavuot is delayed until actual nightfall.

Likewise, all second days of festivals must be ushered in at night, so as not to encroach on the first day of the festival. The second day of Rosh HaShanah, the second day of Sukkot, Simhat Torah (which is actually the second day of Shemini Atzeret), the second and eighth day of Pesah, and the second day of Shavuot are all included in this proviso.

Misconception: Because the observances of Pesah and Sukkot begin only at night, these festivals may not be ushered in earlier than nightfall.

The *mitzvah* of eating in the *sukkah* begins only on the night of the fifteenth day of the month of *Tishray*. Likewise, all observances connected with the Pesah *seder*, including the four cups of wine, telling the story, and eating matzah, must commence only after nightfall.

But this does not mean that the *Yom Tov* itself cannot be ushered in earlier. It is possible, even advisable, to extend the sanctity of these holy days by accepting them earlier, through the evening prayer of *Maariv*.

Then, after starting a festival earlier, one must wait for nightfall to commence with the particular observances linked to those days.

Misconception: During Passover, there is no time when one is forbidden to eat *matzah*.

It is forbidden to eat *matzah* on the day before the beginning of Passover. This is to ensure that we eat the *matzah* with anticipation and greater appetite.

Outside Israel, there is an added caution applicable to the first day of Passover. Because there will be a second *seder*, on the second night, one should likewise avoid *matzah* on the afternoon of the first day of *Pesah*, to ensure a reasonable appetite for *matzah* during the second *seder*.

In addition, the general prohibition against eating bread products close to *Shabbat* or the festival pertains on *Pesah*. This prohibition is to heighten the eagerness for the *Shabbat* or festival meal.

Effectively, then, there are a few times during Pesah when one should not eat *matzah*. They are as follows: the afternoon prior to the second *seder*, the afternoon prior to *Shabbat Hol HaMoed* (Intermediate Days) Pesah, and the afternoon prior to the last day (in Israel) or days (outside Israel) of Pesah.

The afternoon generally refers to the time period beyond the three-quarter mark of the day, namely, beginning three hours before sunset.

184

Misconception: There is no *mitzvah* fulfillment for leavened products on Passover.

Ideally, one should have no involvement with leavened products on Passover. Sometimes, however, the best plans do not work out as anticipated.

Consider the case of one who thinks that all the leaven in the house has been properly disposed of but who is shocked to find a bread roll under the bed during the *Pesah* festival. What should be done?

If it is found on the first two days, it should be covered until the onset of *Hol HaMoed*, the intermediate period buffering the more festive first two days and last two days.

Then, in the intermediate days, this roll, this *hametz* (leaven), is burned. If the one who found the *hametz* had not renounced the leaven prior to Pesah, then the blessing concerning the obligation to get rid of *hametz* is recited.

If the leaven is found in the intermediate days, it is burned immediately, unless the intermediate day is *Shabbat*, in which case the procedure is deferred until the conclusion of the *Shabbat*.

Should the roll be found in the last two days, it is also covered and held until after the conclusion of Pesah, at which time it is burned, but with no blessing recited, because the *mitzvah* of ridding the home of *hametz* terminates with the conclusion of Pesah.

But during Pesah, if *hametz* is found, there is a *mitzvah*, even a pressing imperative, to burn it.

Misconception: There are no special meal requirements on *Hol HaMoed*.

The intermediate days of both Pesah and Sukkot are a combination of ordinary and sacred. They are part of the appointed time and celebration, but they are less demanding in terms of work restrictions. Absolutely necessary work of a certain type is permitted during these days.

However, these days should not be reduced to ordinary days. These are special days, and as such, one is obliged to celebrate the days and their specialness. One must enjoy these days together with the family and others less fortunate, including in them meat, wine, and festive, meaningful spirit.

Hol HaMoed is unfortunately a Jewish affirmation that does not get the respect it deserves — the respect of being an integral part of the *Yom Tov* of Pesah and of Sukkot.

Misconception: No wedding is permitted to take place during *Hol HaMoed*.

As a general rule, weddings are prohibited during times of obligatory joy. This is based on the principle that we do not mix joyous occasions. Rather, we choose to celebrate each occasion on its own, fully and completely.

An exception to this rule is made when a husband and wife who had divorced decide to remarry. Although this law of remarriage is not intended to downplay its significance, it nevertheless is the case that remarriage is less a new reality and more the reestablishment of an old reality.

Because of this, it is permitted on *Hol HaMoed*.

Misconception: One may attach only three *haddasim* (myrtle branches) to the *lulav* (palm branch).

Generally, in instances when the formula for an observance is given, we are obliged to adhere to that formula and not to add thereto or to detract therefrom.

Thus, we cannot add an extra parchment to the *tefillin* encasement or add another corner with fringes to the *tallit*.

However, concerning the three *haddasim*, even though three is the required number, there is no prohibition against adding thereto. As a matter of fact, according to some customs, the entire *lulav* is surrounded with *haddasim*.

One must have a minimum of three, but three is not a maximum number.

The general practice, however, is to bind three *haddasim* and two *aravot* (willows) to the *lulav*.

Misconception: Simhat Torah (joy for completing the Torah cycle) is a separate and independent festival.

Simhat Torah, although it is one of the most joyous days of the Jewish calendar, is not an independent festival.

Instead, Simhat Torah is superimposed upon an already existing festival, namely, Shemini Atzeret (Eighth Day of Assembly).

In Israel, where Shemini Atzeret is one day only, that day also doubles as Simhat Torah. The day of solemn assembly is given an added impetus through its also being the day the Torah cycle is completed.

Outside Israel, Shemini Atzeret is of two days duration, with Simhat Torah integrated into the second day. The joyous atmosphere of the day almost blurs the fact that it is actually Shemini Atzeret. But it is clear that this is the case, because one of the Torah readings for the day is an excerpt about the order of service in the *Bet HaMikdash* on Shemini Atzeret and because in the prayers, the day itself is referred to as Shemini Atzeret.

In essence, it is on Shemini Atzeret, as a day of assembly, that we assemble to glorify God by completing God's Torah and then immediately starting a new cycle of the Torah.

Misconception: After the conclusion of Sukkot, one may throw away the *lulav* and the *etrog*.

The *lulav* and *etrog*, which are employed on Sukkot for the purpose of fulfilling a *mitzvah*, retain a special sanctity even after the Festival.

An item with which a *mitzvah* has been achieved should not at any point in time be treated as ordinary. It cannot become an item to be thrown into the garbage. It should be treated with respect.

Many have the custom of holding the *lulav* and its branches of myrtles and willows until just before Passover, when it forms part of the fire that will be made to burn the *hametz* (leavened) products.

The logic informing this custom is that an item that has been used to fulfill one *mitzvah* (in this instance, one connected with Sukkot) should be used to fulfill another *mitzvah* (in this instance, one associated with pre-Pesah obligations).

Misconception: After setting an *eruv tavshilin*, one may prepare food on any of the *Yom Tov* days for *Shabbat*.

When a festival precedes the *Shabbat*, there is a problem related to food preparation for *Shabbat*. Normally, one may not prepare on any Yom Tov day for a day beyond, whether it be the next day of *Yom Tov* or a weekday or even, under normal circumstances, *Shabbat*.

With regard to *Shabbat*, this poses serious problems, because the prohibition against such preparation would make it almost impossible to properly celebrate the *Shabbat*.

It is for this reason that the sages created a form of continuity between the *Yom Tov* and the *Shabbat*, through what is referred to as an *eruv tavshilin* — a bringing together, or mixing, of the foodstuffs.

One sets aside a baked item, such as bread, and a cooked item, such as fish or meat or an egg, and recites the proper formula, prior to the *Yom Tov*, that will create some continuity of food preparation. Through this mechanism, one may prepare on the Friday of the festival for the *Shabbat*. This permissibility pertains only to preparing on the Friday of the festival for the *Shabbat*. However, if the two-day festival begins on Thursday, one may not prepare on the Thursday for the *Shabbat*.

It is only on the Friday that one may prepare for the *Shabbat*. This continuity culminates on *Shabbat* with one's eating the two foods that were set aside prior to the festival.

Misconception: In preparing food on the Friday of a festival for *Shabbat*, the later the preparations, the better.

The effectiveness of the mechanism for allowing food preparation on the Friday of a *Yom Tov* for *Shabbat* pertains only under very precise conditions.

One may prepare on the Friday for the *Shabbat* only if the food is prepared with enough time left in the day so that if guests arrive who have not yet eaten, they will still have time before *Shabbat* to enjoy from the food that is prepared.

Even though the food is prepared for *Shabbat*, technically it still must be available to be eaten on the festival day itself. If the food is prepared in such a time frame that it cannot be eaten on the festival day, that is unacceptable. It is only when technically the food could still be eaten on the *Yom Tov* day itself that one is allowed to use it for the *Shabbat*.

The sages were very careful, in allowing for the carryover into the *Shabbat*, not to compromise the sanctity of the festival, while they were sensitive to the obvious concern with having fresh foodstuff available for the *Shabbat*.

Misconception: The custom of reciting *Yizkor* (the remembrance prayer) on the festivals has always been a unanimously endorsed practice.

Yizkor has become a basic staple of the festivals. It is recited on the last day of Pesah and Shavuot, on Shemini Atzeret, and on Yom Kippur.

However, before this became accepted practice on a universal scale, it went through an intense period of debate. Some sages felt that the recitation of a memorial prayer was inconsistent with the spirit of joy that should dominate the festivals. Their objections notwithstanding, *Yizkor* has become part of the prayer service on the festivals and on Yom Kippur.

The basic reasoning for this was that the community was more likely to be present on these days, and therefore it would be an opportune time to recall the memory of loved ones who were martyred.

The integration of this remembrance into a day of joy served to solemnize the joy into a more serious, sober appreciation of life rather than merely a euphoric, unrealistic, and self-indulgent celebration.

Misconception: There are no special rules regarding letter-writing in the month of *Elul*.

Elul is the month immediately prior to Rosh HaShanah and the ensuing ten days of repentance. As the prelude to this critical period, it is a time when we warm up to the penitential obligations related to these ten days. Because the Rosh HaShanah period is the time when our fate is decided, we become sensitive to this in the month prior to Rosh HaShanah.

Part of that sensitivity is exhibited through our ongoing concern for the welfare of our family and friends. This should be expressed whenever meeting such friends.

In addition, when writing a letter during this period, one should include in it the wishes we have for our friends, that they be blessed with a fulfilling and healthful year.

The month before Rosh HaShanah is no ordinary month, and the letters we write are no ordinary letters. They must include our awareness of and sensitivity to the people we hold dear.

Misconception: *LeShanah Tovah* is the correct greeting to extend to others on Rosh HaShanah.

On Rosh HaShanah, we extend our best wishes to those we meet through the formula for having a good year.

There are two possible variations of the formula: one is *LeShanah Tovah Tikatayvu veTayhataymu* (for males) and *LeShanah Tovah Tikatayvi veTayhataymi* (for females). Translated, they mean, "You should be written and inscribed for a good year."

The other alternative is to generally extend the more simple wish, *Shanah Tovah*. This translates as, "Have a good year."

However, *LeShanah Tovah* is neither here nor there. Its direct translation is, "for a good year." But this leaves things in limbo. For a good year . . . what? It tries to combine the two greetings in a way that does not accurately convey the sense of either.

Undoubtedly, the sentiment is honest and genuine, but the carry-through is less than accurate.

Because we are seriously concerned about the welfare of others, that seriousness should reflect itself by being sure the greeting we extend is as accurate as the seriousness with which it is intended.

Misconception: The *shofar* was never blown on Rosh HaShanah that occurred on *Shabbat*.

It is common practice not to blow the *shofar* on the *Shabbat* on which Rosh HaShanah occurs.

However, this was not always the case. The rabbinic edict forbidding the blowing of the *shofar* on Rosh HaShanah came as a reaction to circumstance, to the fear that through blowing the *shofar* on Rosh HaShanah, there would be a serious value distortion.

This value distortion resulted from placing so much emphasis on the *shofar* that *Shabbat* protocols, such as refraining from carrying in a public domain, were neglected. Because *Shabbat* involves so many prohibitions, and their breach is so serious, it did not make sense to allow even for as meaningful a fulfillment as the blowing of the *shofar*, if realized through *Shabbat* desecration.

It hardly makes sense to be awakened to penitence by doing that which is prohibited. But this was all rabbinic enactment—wise enactment, yet postbiblical enactment. Even so, for some time, the *shofar* was actually blown on Rosh HaShanah, especially in the *Bet HaMikdash*. And in the *Bet Din* of Rabbenu Yitzhak Alfasi, popularly known as RIF, who lived in Morocco and Spain in the eleventh century, the shofar was blown on Rosh HaShanah that occurred on *Shabbat*.

Misconception: It is forbidden to sleep on Rosh HaShanah afternoon.

It is customary to stay awake on Rosh HaShanah afternoon. Some are under the impression that this staying awake is obligatory. It is grounded in the oft-quoted rabbinic comment that for one who sleeps, that person's *mazal* (destiny) also sleeps.

But this is based on a faulty translation. The exact statement that is the ostensible basis for the practice reads as follows: One who dies on Rosh HaShanah, that person's *mazal* died. This refers to the notion that the demise had been preordained from last year. It says nothing about having to stay awake.

There is even some doubt as to whether the text about having to stay awake actually exists.

It is fitting to be awake on Rosh HaShanah afternoon and to use the time for useful endeavors, such as study and prayer. But, as is stated with such impact in the codes, one who is idle in this time is considered asleep (at the switch). And those who, in order to stay awake on Rosh HaShanah afternoon, opt for spending the time with their friends in idle gossip and chatter, have missed the point in a more serious way.

If the only choices available to an individual on Rosh HaShanah afternoon are idle gossip or sleeping, sleeping is the preferable alternative.

Obviously, other options are available. Those options, meaningful options related to the purpose of Rosh HaShanah, should be embraced.

Misconception: The custom of *kaparot* prior to Yom Kippur has always been well received.

Although it is now a well-entrenched practice to engage in the *kaparot* ritual on the day prior to Yom Kippur, this practice originally met with vehement opposition. There were sages who felt it was an ill-advised practice because it smacked of scapegoating, of placing one's spiritual deficits onto a poor chicken and thereby somehow magically inducing expiation. This is superstition and certainly not consistent with Jewish tradition.

Despite the opposition, the custom has prevailed, but it has taken many twists. The opposition did serve to give it a clearer focus. That focus is on the actual *kaparot* ceremony's being a catalyst for repentance but not the actual expression of repentance.

In addition, the act itself has been ennobled to be one of charitable benefit. The chicken is given to the poor, or the money that is used for it is directed toward charity.

Thus, *kaparot* has become a way of creating the proper mood of empathy on Yom Kippur, by entrenching the charity focus on the day prior to Yom Kippur.

Misconception: *Kol Nidray* has always been a popular statement.

Kol Nidray, the by now famous statement renouncing vows, is the opening expression of Yom Kippur. But it is not a prayer devoid of controversy. Not only was there controversy regarding the text (whether, for example, the renunciation should be of past or future vows) but there was also controversy regarding the basic statement.

Some attribute the objection to it to possible innovations by mystics who saw it as a neutralization of a magical fear of vows. Some felt that public renunciation of vows would be distorted as proof positive that Jews can never be trusted, since any promise they may make they almost immediately nullify. According to some, the major concern addressed by *Kol Nidray* was the forced commitment to another faith that many Jews were coerced into, on pain of death. This promise was renounced on Yom Kippur. But as for other promises, truth and justice must prevail.

Insofar as maintaining *Kol Nidray* in the liturgy, justice did indeed prevail.

Misconception: Yom Kippur is a sad day.

Yom Kippur is anything but a sad day. One of the suggested reasons we wear a white garment, called *kittel*, on Yom Kippur is to project the idea that we approach this day in optimism and joy, hopeful for the best heavenly verdict regarding our fate — to be given a clean, white slate.

We do not mourn, we do not lament. On the contrary, we rejoice in the notion that repentance is made available to us, to thereby absolve us of past iniquity.

Yom Kippur has all the trimmings of a festival, with the only difference being that it is a festival in which our full and total concentration is on the purpose of the day. We do not eat and we do not engage in any worldly delights. But we do engage in the spiritual delight of self-improvement and resolution for the future.

In the words of the Talmud, Yom Kippur was one of the happiest days in the Jewish calendar. And so should it continue to be.

Misconception: The Maccabees lit a Hanukah *menorah* to reestablish the *Bet HaMikdash*.

Many people derive from the fact that we kindle a Hanukah *menorah* to recall the miracle of the oil that the Maccabees of yesteryear kindled a similar *menorah* when they reentered the sanctuary.

Ironically, this is not the case. The Maccabees lit the eternal light of the *menorah* that was to burn continuously for twenty-four hours without break and without interruption.

They had oil to light this eternal light only for one day, but miraculously the oil sustained the light for eight days, enough time for a fresh supply of oil to reach the sanctuary and maintain the process of continuous lighting. The Maccabees did not light a Hanukah *menorah*; they lit the *menorah* of seven lights. We light a *hanukiah* (Hanukah *menorah*) to recall that the Maccabees lit the eternal flame.

How the recollection of the miracle deviated from the original miracle is in itself quite interesting. We recall, but we do not reenact. The idea of the eternal is particular to the *Bet HaMikdash*, and we dare not blur the boundary between the Holy Sanctuary and ordinary abodes. We cannot do exactly as was done in the *Bet HaMikdash*.

Therefore, the obligation is not to light a flame that lasts twenty-four hours. We kindle a flame that lasts for just half an hour, enough time to be significant as recollection.

Our kindling differs from the Maccabean kindling in yet another way: we move from one flame on the first night, increasing every night and culminating with eight flames by the eighth and last night.

This is to impress upon us the obligation not to remain static in our spiritual quest but to make every day of that spiritual quest better than the day before and not as good as the day to come.

Particularly with reference to Hanukah, it is our charge to spread the light of Judaism into Judaic homes that have been bereft of that light, to forestall the type of assimilation that in fact was quite manifest in the period prior to Hanukah and that threatened the Jewish people of yesteryear.

Misconception: The main target audience for publicizing the miracle of Hanukah is the non-Jewish population.

Wrong. Hanukah is not a festival for non-Jews; it is a festival for Jews. There is no obligation for non-Jews to celebrate Hanukah or to participate in its celebration.

Recent attempts to escalate Hanukah into a national observance, with candlelighting ceremonies on the grounds of legislatures or parliaments, project the idea of Hanukah as a nationalistic expression. This is a distortion of Hanukah. Hanukah is the celebration of a theological deliverance; it is a religious festival. It is wrong for Jews to impose their religious observance on others.

When it comes to publicizing the miracle, such publicizing is for the emendation and inspiration of members of the Jewish community, who should be inspired by the *hanukiah* to contemplate the true meaning of Hanukah and to thereby gain a greater appreciation of God.

Misconception: Hanukah is primarily a cultural celebration.

There has been a tendency, at least in America, to see Hanukah as something it is not, namely, an alternative cultural expression for Jews or a counterpart of the festive expressions of other groups.

Some feel it is the identity expression that is needed to withstand the onslaught that threatens to engulf Jews in an avalanche of non-Jewish holiday spirit. They have their holiday and we have ours. In order to broadcast this with full force, we tend to exhibit the *hanukiah*, the Hanukah *menorah*, as the alternative to the other lights that adorn a tree, a bush, or whatever.

Hanukah is celebrated by an overwhelming majority of Jews, however assimilated. To deny that Hanukah serves some form of cultural usefulness, in terms of providing a mode of identity expression, would be preposterous. It would be to deny a reality that stares us in the eye.

It is one thing to deny a reality; it is another to affirm the legitimacy of that reality. Hanukah is used as a mode of ethnic or cultural expression, but that is not what it was in its original form, nor is it what is intended in its present form.

Hanukah celebrates the victory over forces that would have denied Jews the right to live as Jews, the right to study Torah, the right to maintain circumcision, the right to maintain a Jewish calendar.

To affirm Hanukah on a once-a-year basis today while at the same time failing to study Torah or failing to go by the Jewish calendar of observances and fulfillments is effectively to distort what Hanukah was, what Hanukah is, what Hanukah should be.

Misconception: It is appropriate to extend the greeting *Hag Sameah* on Hanukah.

Hag Sameah, which translates loosely as, "Have a joyous festival," is a greeting associated with various festival occasions.

However, these are all festive occasions rooted in biblical mandate. Therefore, it is appropriate to extend the greeting *Hag Sameah* for Pesah (on Pesah one actually adds *Hag Kasher veSameah*), Shavuot, and Sukkot, all biblically referred to as *hag*, festival. However, to extend the greeting *Hag Sameah* for Hanukah would thereby place Hanukah on a par with these other major festivals.

Hanukah is not a major festival; it is a minor, nonbiblical festival. One must always retain perspective, in spite of the social pressures to the contrary.

It is appropriate to extend the greeting *Hag Urim Sameah*, which is, "Have a joyous Festival of Lights," or to simply say, "Hanukah *Sameah*," Happy Hanukah. But the greeting must be distinctive and indigenous to Hanukah and not the parroting of a greeting that is reserved for the major festivals of the Jewish calendar.

Misconception: The *Sheheheyanu* blessing on Hanukah may be recited only on the first night.

The *Sheheheyanu* blessing, extolling God "for having sustained us, to reach this time," is a blessing of joy. Under normal circumstances, it is recited at the first instance of a fulfillment or an event.

With regard to Hanukah, the first and most appropriate time to recite this blessing is on the first night, when reciting the benedictions for the kindling of the Hanukah lights.

However, there are times when this blessing may be recited at a later juncture during Hanukah. One may have been unable to kindle the Hanukah lights on the first night, or the second, or simply may have forgotten to recite this blessing.

In such situations, one recites the *Sheheheyanu* blessing on the first occasion when the Hanukah lights are kindled, but obviously the sooner the better or, in the case of forgetfulness, on the first occasion one remembers to do so.

Misconception: There is no difference in the kindling of Hanukah lights on Friday prior to the *Shabbat*.

The kindling of the Hanukah lights prior to the *Shabbat* poses a particular problem. *Shabbat* is ushered in eighteen minutes before sunset, and the Hanukah lights must be aflame for half an hour after the beginning of the night. Add together the eighteen minutes before sunset, the forty-two minutes between sunset and nighttime, and another half an hour, and it becomes clear that the Hanukah lights must burn for at least an hour and a half on Friday evening.

Effectively, this translates into a little more than that, because one must light the Hanukah candles more than eighteen minutes before *Shabbat*, in order to allow time for the *Shabbat* candles to be lit.

The procedure, then, on Friday evening, is to kindle the Hanukah lights before kindling the *Shabbat* lights. And the Hanukah lights, if of oil, must have sufficient oil to last for more than one and a half hours. If candles are used, they cannot be the ordinary candles employed for Hanukah, since these usually last no more than about forty minutes.

Ironically, in this instance the candles should be of the *Shabbat*-candle type, or those specially produced, long-kindling Hanukah candles, which last for the necessary time.

Misconception: All *dreidels* have the same letters.

Outside Israel, the toy top, called *dreidel*, which is played on Hanukah, has four specific letters. They are *nun*, *gimmel*, *heh*, and *shin*. Together, they signify *nes gadol hayah sham*, meaning, "a great miracle occurred there [in Israel]."

Israeli *dreidels* have a slight adjustment to this significant statement. Israeli *dreidels* contain the letters *nun*, *gimmel*, *heh*, and *peh*. Together, they signify *nes gadol hayah poh*, "a great miracle occurred here."

Misconception: *Dreidel*-playing and other games of chance capture the true meaning and spirit of Hanukah.

Hanukah celebrates the first victory in history against religious persecution and denial of religious freedom.

The oppressors of the Jews forbade them the study of the Torah and various Jewish affirmations. If Jews were caught studying Torah, for example, their lives were imperiled.

In order to avoid this threat of death while continuing to study, they would have gambling instruments available on the table so that if soldiers barged into the room, they would make believe they were playing. In reality, they were studying Torah.

If we would like to recapture the spirit of Hanukah, it is not through *dreidel*-playing. That was just a camouflage for the essence of the conflict and of the resistance of Israel to oppression. Jews resisted because they wanted the freedom to study and live the Torah.

We in our generation can best celebrate Hanukah by studying the very Torah that inspired the Maccabees of old to risk their lives. Anything else misses the point of Hanukah.

Misconception: All leftover oil from Hanukah may be used or reused.

On occasion, the oil one places in the *hanukiah* may not be totally used up. The wick may have been extinguished with some oil still remaining. The oil that is left over during Hanukah should be carried over to the next day's kindling.

But what about the oil that is left over after the last day? That oil should not be used for ordinary, non-*mitzvah* purposes, because it has been designated for the *mitzvah* of kindling the Hanukah lights. It must be disposed of respectfully.

However, there is a way to avoid the problem of leftover oil. It is achieved by stating, before using the oil, that only the oil consumed by the wicks is designated for the *mitzvah* but that any other oil is not. Thus the leftover oil is considered ordinary oil and may be used for any legitimate purpose.

This may seem like a big deal for a little oil, but it projects some vital values within Judaism. Those values involve both the sanctity of that which is designated for sacred purposes and the importance of conservation, even conservation of items of very small measure.

Misconception: Sending *manot* (food items) to others is the main person-to-person fulfillment on Purim.

There are a number of obligation fulfillments attendant to Purim. One, of course, is the praise of God that emanates from the recitation of *Megillat Esther*, which recounts the story of Purim. Another is the sending of food items to others. Finally, there is the sending of gifts or money to the poor.

The money that is given to the poor is to help them celebrate Purim. It is assumed that the poor do not have the money for anything other than meager subsistence.

Purim is a day on which the entire community must experience the joy of redemption. We show our sensitivity to the poor by helping them to be part of this great communal celebration.

It is this giving to the poor, this combination of sensitivity and community togetherness, that is the key element in the person-to-person fulfillments on Purim.

Misconception: Women are not obligated in the matter of *Mishlo'ah Manot* on Purim.

It is a mistake to believe that women are not obliged to send *manot* on Purim. Even though any fulfillment associated with Purim is a fulfillment that is contingent on a specific time, and under normal circumstances women are exempt from fulfilling time-related precepts, Purim is one of the exceptions.

Women were as much in peril as men in the period prior to Purim, and the actual deliverance was effected through Esther, herself a woman. Women are as intricate a component of the community as men, and the deliverance we celebrate is a celebration of the deliverance of both the men and the women.

Therefore, both men and women are obligated in all the fulfillments associated with Purim, including the sending of *manot* to others, giving to the poor, and of course listening to the story as told in *Megillat Esther*.

Misconception: *Rosh Hodesh* is always the first day of the new month.

Thus it would seem, since, after all, the word *rosh* means "head" and *hodesh* means "month." This translates as "head of the month," or "first day."

However, this is not always the case. When *Rosh Hodesh* is only one day, indeed that day is the first day of the new month. When *Rosh Hodesh* is two days, the first day of *Rosh Hodesh* is the thirtieth day of the previous month, and the second day of *Rosh Hodesh* is the first day of the new month.

When *Rosh Hodesh* is two days, the previous month is of thirty days duration. Or, put the opposite way, in a month that is of thirty days duration, the last day is *Rosh Hodesh*.

When *Rosh Hodesh* is one day, the previous month is twenty-nine days. Put the other way, when a month is twenty-nine days, the *Rosh Hodesh* for the next month comes after the twenty-nine days.

A lunar month is slightly more than twenty-nine and a half days. The challenge is what to do with the half-day.

It is of course ill advised to have a day that is half *Rosh Hodesh* and half not. For balance purposes, we adjust the length of the months. Some months are twenty-nine days, and the other months are thirty days.

In a thirty-day month, the last half of the thirtieth day is already part of the next month in technical terms — in fact, the head of the month, *Rosh Hodesh*. Therefore, that entire day is designated as *Rosh Hodesh*.

Misconception: The fifteenth day of the month is always too late to recite the *Kiddush Levanah*.

Kiddush Levanah is a profound service expressing our appreciation to God for the majesty of creation and the cosmological order God has entrenched, including the regular lunar cycle.

This prayer is recited monthly, in the first part of the month, after the first few days, and before the middle of the month, when the moon starts to downsize.

One would expect that by the fifteenth day, the halfway point in the month has arrived. However, the key issue regarding *Kiddush Levanah* is the halfway point of time in the month, starting from the precise birth of the new moon. This is announced in the *Bet Knesset* when the prayer that ushers in the new moon is recited.

Because a month is about twenty-nine days and twelve hours-plus, one can recite the *Kiddush Levanah* until exactly one half of this time period, or about fourteen days and eighteen-plus hours.

This can extend into the night of the fifteenth or even the sixteenth day of the month. For example, if the start of the new moon is in early afternoon, one may be able to recite the *Kiddush Levanah* on the night of the fifteenth, or later, as the case may be.

Misconception: One may recite the *Kiddush Levanah* only after seven days.

In reality, after three full days from the precise birth of the month, one can recite *Kiddush Levanah*. After three days, one already gains some luminous benefit from the moon. This justifies reciting the *Kiddush Levanah* blessing.

Since this is justified after three days, it is then preferable to fulfill this obligation as early as possible and not squander the opportunity for a fulfillment by waiting for the seventh day.

According to some, this is the case even if the post-three-days, pre-seven-days opportunity occurs on a weekday, prior to *Motzaay Shabbat* (Saturday night), *Motzaay Shabbat* being the ideal time for *Kiddush Levanah*. It is ideal because more are likely to attend, and they are dressed in their *Shabbat* clothing. All this enhances the fulfillment.

Fulfilling a precept at the earliest possible time is the overriding consideration. This is especially so in wintry or rainy seasons, when one cannot be sure the moon will be visible later on.

Misconception: Yom HaAtzmaut is a secular occasion.

Yom HaAtzmaut celebrates the day that Israel became an independent state. To this day, there are extremist groups within Judaism, on opposite sides of the spectrum, that do not recognize either Israel or its significance. But the overwhelming majority in between have a full and abiding appreciation of what Israel means to the Jewish people. There is also an ongoing debate as to whether the reestablishment of the state signals the dawn of redemption.

Whatever future implications there may be for the present existence of the State of Israel, there is no question that the rebirth of the state has engendered a rejuvenation of Jewish learning and of the Jewish spirit, in a way and in a proportion that are literally mind-boggling.

What the original founders of the state may have had in mind is irrelevant. The outgrowth of the creation of the state has resulted not only in a spiritual revival but also, as had been hoped for, in the opportunity to save the remnant of Israel, wherever they may be, from persecution and possible annihilation.

All of this provides more than ample reason to celebrate the rebirth of the State of Israel, not merely as a secular occasion but also as a profoundly religious and momentous event.

10

Not-So-Happy Days

Misconception: The *Omer* period, between Pesah and Shavuot, has always been a sad period.

Originally, the *Omer* period, as described in the Torah, connected the festival of freedom — Pesah — with the festival of responsibility — Shavuot. *Omer* links these two celebrations and thereby establishes that our concept of freedom is freedom toward the embracing of God's Torah as our way of life.

This was to be a happy period, linking two great festivals and building to a crescendo of anticipation from the one toward the other. However, Jewish history has given a different coloration to this period. It was a time when thousands of the students of Rabbi Akiva died. It was also undoubtedly a period when the post-Pesah blood libels invaded and destroyed whatever tranquillity the Jewish people may have had in their turbulent period of existence in exile.

History has transmuted what had been designed to be a joyous period into one of sadness.

Misconception: It is prohibited to listen to any music during the semimourning period between Pesah and Shavuot.

The semimourning period of thirty-three days, in the forty-nine days between Pesah and Shavuot, carries with it some concrete restrictions, including the prohibition against marriage ceremonies during that time.

It has been commonly assumed that music is prohibited during this time. However, it is wrong to put all music in the same category. Obviously, happiness-inducing music, such as the dance music that is associated with weddings, is proscribed. But there are other types of music, including the type of background, relaxing music that is not for joy and happiness — neither in its intent nor in its content. Such music poses no problem during this period of time. There is no rule prohibiting relaxation even in this thirty-three day period. There is a prohibition against being ecstatically happy, as one might be during a wedding. But to contentedly listen to classical or soft music in the privacy of one's home is permissible.

It is important to keep this in perspective, to know the precise lines separating permissible from prohibited, rather than to blur the lines and thereby create prohibitions that do not exist.

Misconception: One may not attend a wedding that occurs during that thirty-three-day segment of semimourning between Pesah and Shavuot that the invitee observes.

There are varying customs regarding the thirty-three-day period of semimourning between Pesah and Shavuot. One custom is to maintain the first thirty-three days of that forty-nine-day period as semimourning.

Another custom is to maintain the last (more or less) thirty-three days as semimourning.

Because only thirty-three days of the seven weeks are to be considered mournful, there are approximately sixteen days at the start and conclusion of this time when differing groups within the community will have divergent practices.

One may possibly be invited to a wedding in any of these days by a family whose custom allows for such celebration.

The guest, whose accepted custom would not allow for actually hosting such an event, may nevertheless attend the wedding.

Misconception: It is wrong to finalize an engagement in the *Omer* period between Pesah and Shavuot.

At least thirty-three days within the *Omer* period between Pesah and Shavuot are days in which festive events such as weddings should not take place.

But the finalization of an engagement, however happy a moment it is, is not in the same category. Weddings are subject to scheduling and should be set for the appropriate time to celebrate.

Engagements are associated more with agreeing to marry through engaging. These are subject to the spontaneity of an unfolding relationship.

It is eminently correct to concretize this agreement at the earliest possible stage, avoiding any delay or repercussions that may ensue from that delay.

Therefore, should such an occasion present itself, even in the period between Pesah and Shavuot, when weddings are off limits, an engagement should be finalized.

Misconception: One may never give a direct answer to one who asks, What day of the *Omer* is it tonight?

Pesah and Shavuot are connected through the counting of the *Omer*, for a seven-week period. Each night, just after nightfall, one recites a blessing and then states what day of the *Omer* it is.

Twilight, the time period between sundown and nightfall, is not clearly established as being day or night and may actually be either one. This is a matter of doubt. Therefore, one should not recite the *Omer* blessing at that time because the twilight may be part of the day.

On the other hand, if one states the *Omer* date in twilight, without reciting a blessing, the blessing for that day can no longer be recited.

The reason for this is that because twilight may belong to the night, the recitation of the date may actually be effective, thus fulfilling the *mitzvah* obligation to count for that day. This would make any blessing for the *mitzvah* unnecessary. Pronouncing an unnecessary blessing is a serious breach, involving the evoking of God's name in vain.

Thus, if asked, in twilight time, what is the *Omer* count for tonight, a straight answer, such as, "Tonight is the sixth day of the *Omer*," is, however unintended, a proper counting. This deprives the person answering of the ability to recite the blessing for counting the *Omer* later on.

It is therefore preferable, when being asked what the *Omer* count is, to give an indirect answer, such as, "Yesterday was the fifth night."

All this applies only to the case of being asked in twilight or at night prior to having recited the blessing. However, once having properly fulfilled the obligation to count with the prior blessing, or before twilight, a direct and precise answer may be given to one who asks what the *Omer* count is for tonight.

Misconception: Insofar as haircuts are concerned, there is no difference when Lag B'Omer (thirty-third day of the *Omer* period between Pesah and Shavuot) occurs.

Haircuts are prohibited during thirty-three of the forty-nine-days between the second day of Pesah and Shavuot. There are varying customs as to which of these thirty-three days are prohibited, with one major custom observing the first thirty-three days and the other the latter thirty-three days of this forty-nine-day period.

The thirty-third day, or Lag (L, *lamed* = 30, G, *gimmel* = 3) B'Omer, is a festive occasion and universally accepted as an appropriate time for haircuts.

The only difference is that for those observing the first custom of the first thirty-three days, haircutting would be permitted only on Lag B'Omer morning, whereas those who follow the latter customs would be permitted to cut their hair from nightfall on Lag B'Omer.

However, should Lag B'Omer occur on a Sunday, whatever the custom, the observance makes a very significant adjustment. When Lag B'Omer falls on a Sunday, one is permitted to have a haircut on the previous Friday. The reason for this is that in order to honor the *Shabbat*, one may cut one's hair on the Friday.

To put this in more precise terms, waiting until Sunday to cut one's hair and look well groomed would be disrespectful to the *Shabbat*. The observance of the prohibition against haircutting is important, but not showing disrespect to *Shabbat* is even more important.

A haircut on a Friday is allowed to avoid the incongruity of waiting until just after the *Shabbat* in order to groom oneself properly.

Misconception: Aside from *Shabbat*, the festivals, and other proscribed times, any day is okay for having one's hair cut.

There are times when it is prohibited to have one's hair cut, such as on *Shabbat* and the festivals. There are other times when having one's hair cut is not as serious a breach as when done on *Shabbat* and *yom tov* but nevertheless should be avoided.

For example, it would be a disparagement of the *Shabbat* to cut one's hair on Sunday or Monday. This would be a turning away from the obligation to make oneself as presentable as possible for the *Shabbat* or the festivals.

It is likewise appropriate to time one's haircut for as close to the *Shabbat* or the festival as possible, in order that this beautification exercise be part of the pre-*Shabbat* or prefestival preparations. This is a significant gesture toward enhancing those days.

Misconception: Listening to music is the primary prohibition in the three weeks between the Fast of the Seventeenth of *Tamuz* and the Fast of the Ninth of *Av*.

The primary thrust during the three-week period between the seventeenth of *Tamuz* and the ninth of *Av* is to create a climate of semimourning and to contemplate the trauma that was endured by our ancestors, the implications of which remain today.

It is not music that is the primary prohibition during this period. The primary prohibition is any celebration or enjoyment that is nonconducive to the mournful contemplation mandatory for the time period.

By placing all the prohibition eggs into the music basket, one unfortunately sounds the wrong note about what this three-week period should mean.

Misconception: There is no reason to avoid a pleasure trip in the three weeks between the Fast of the Seventeenth of *Tamuz* and the Fast of the Ninth of *Av*.

The three-week period between the Fast of the Seventeenth of *Tamuz* and the Fast of the Ninth of *Av* is a period of melancholy. It is a time for sober reflection on the fate of the Jewish people of yesteryear and the continuing impact of the tragic events of thousands of years ago.

In the public mind, this three-week period is associated primarily with no weddings, no joyous music, and no partying. But there is more to the three weeks than this. The three weeks is a contemplative and sober period, not a time to engage in worldly pleasures.

A pleasure trip during this time is out-of-bounds, even more so in the more intense mourning period of the last nine days of these three weeks. A pleasure trip is as much a distancing from the obligation to contemplate our history as are other, more radical forms of distancing. In fact, a pleasure trip may even be worse in that it is protracted over a longer period and is therefore a much more serious deviation.

Misconception: It is a universal rule that no weddings are permitted in the three weeks.

The three weeks refers to the mourning period between the seventeenth day of *Tamuz* and the ninth day of *Av*. On the seventeenth day of *Tamuz*, the first breach was made in the walls of Jerusalem. This signaled both the beginning of the end for the Holy City and the destruction of the *Bet HaMikdash*, which was to follow.

On Tishah B'Av (Ninth Day of *Av*) itself, the *Bet HaMikdash* was destroyed. This destruction was the culmination of tremendous loss of life and great tragedies in the Jewish community in Israel. It also signaled the beginning of exile and the loss of autonomy.

The custom that has developed over the years is to commemorate and recall this terrible period in our history by refraining from having any weddings. However, Sephardic custom allows weddings in this three-week period, until but not including *Rosh Hodesh Av*. One can justify this by the logic that we specifically go out of our way in this period of national tragedy to show that we have faith in the future return. Precisely in the time of tragedy do we engage in rebuilding by establishing the building blocks of communal life through marriage.

This is the basic law among Sephardim. However, in general practice, the Sephardim do not nowadays schedule weddings for the three-week period. This is an act of community solidarity on their part. It is their way of showing concern for the Ashkenazic community and sensitivity to Ashkenazic practice.

Misconception: All people are forbidden to shave or cut their hair in the three-week period between the seventeenth of *Tamuz* and the ninth of *Av*.

The three-week period between the seventeenth of *Tamuz* and the ninth of *Av* is a period of semimourning, escalating toward the end to more intense mourning and culminating with full-fledged mourning on Tishah B'Av itself.

Under normal circumstances, haircuts and shaving are prohibited during this time period.

However, someone who has suffered the loss of one of the five relatives other than parents (brother, sister, wife, son, or daughter) and enters into the three-week period with no intervening time from the conclusion of the thirty-day mourning period to the start of the three-week mourning period is given special consideration.

Such an individual, if not allowed a shave or haircut for another three weeks, would have the burden of a protracted time period of not shaving or cutting the hair. Such an individual is allowed to shave or have a haircut during the three-week period prior to *Rosh Hodesh Av*, when the more intense mourning period called "The Nine Days" begins.

It is the exception to the rule, an exception that shows particular understanding for an individual who has suffered a trauma and is therefore not given what would amount to an extra burden to bear.

In addition, the main participants in a circumcision — the father, the one holding the baby during circumcision (*sandek*), and the one performing the circumcision (*mohel*) — may cut their hair in honor of a *brit milah* (covenantal circumcision) that takes place before *Rosh Hodesh Av*.

Misconception: Showering in the nine-day period prior to the Fast of Tishah B'Av is forbidden.

Generally, it is best to avoid showering in the nine-day period prior to the Fast of Tishah B'Av. This is part of the general mourning practices that prevail during this melancholy period in the Jewish calendar, just prior to the commemoration of the destruction of both Temples, which occurred on Tishah B'Av.

Certainly, showering for the pure pleasure of taking a shower would be out-of-bounds during this period. However, especially for those people who live in warmer climates, going nine days without cleansing the body may be unduly oppressive — not only for those not showering but also for all those in the immediate vicinity of such individuals, who may well be repelled by the olfactory implications of such lack of showering.

Therefore, even in this nine-day period, one may take a quick shower to cleanse oneself. But it is important to keep the boundaries clear, to always be aware of the reason one is showering, and therefore to do so with greater dispatch.

Misconception: Tishah B'Av is simply a fast day with no work
prohibitions.

Tishah B'Av, commemorating the destruction of the first and
second *Bet HaMikdash,* is a day of intense mourning.

Primarily, the mourning focuses on the Book of Lamentations,
called *Aykhah,* and on the elegies, the *kinot,* which are particular to
Tishah B'Av and to other tragedies that have befallen the Jewish
people over the course of the generations. These are tragedies that
were the direct result of protracted exile and vulnerability and are
therefore more than symbolically linked with Tishah B'Av itself.

If Tishah B'Av is to be spent in intense mourning, it hardly
makes sense that one should be involved in any work. It is thus
understandable that Tishah B'Av is not a day on which working is
appropriate.

Nevertheless, in extenuating circumstances, some form of
activity is reluctantly permitted from midday of Tishah B'Av itself.
But even that is not at all recommended. If at all possible, it should
be avoided.

Misconception: Tishah B'Av is not a *yom tov*.

Tishah B'Av is the mournful fast commemorating the destruction of the two Temples and the thrusting of Israel into exile. This is hardly a *yom tov* — a good day.

However, strange as it may seem, Tishah B'av is called a *mo'ed* (a point in time, a happy time). There is even manifestation of this on Tishah B'Av itself, in that the *Tahanun* (supplication) prayer omitted on festivals is not recited.

How can Tishah B'Av be simultaneously the most mournful day in the year and also a happy time? Does this not smack of theological schizophrenia?

The simple answer is that although Tishah B'Av is the most mournful day in the Jewish calendar, we hope the mourning will eventually turn into celebration. This is in line with the prophecy of Zekharyah, that Tishah B'Av will eventually become a *yom tov*, a celebrative day.

We have never given up hope for our return to Jerusalem and the reestablishment of the *Bet HaMikdash*. This idea is encapsulated in the famous notion that the Messiah was born on Tishah B'Av.

In a metaphoric sense, the hope for salvation is born when one reaches rock bottom. When there is no way to go but up, the proper reflex is not to give up but to say that things can only get better and that they will get better.

Thus, the deepest throes of despair create within themselves the potential for redemption. Tishah B'Av is indeed the harbinger for *yom tov*, for good days ahead.

Misconception: Physical contact between husband and wife is forbidden the entire day of Tishah B'Av.

Tishah B'Av, like Yom Kippur, is a day on which conjugal visitation between husband and wife is prohibited. It is a day of mourning, national mourning of an intense nature. Conjugal union is inconsistent with the mood of melancholy that should prevail on Tishah B'Av.

However, insofar as physical contact is concerned, it is permitted following midday of Tishah B'Av itself. In this respect, Tishah B'Av differs from Yom Kippur, wherein such physical contact is proscribed for the entire day.

232

Misconception: All running shoes are acceptable wear for Yom Kippur and Tishah B'Av.

It is well known that shoes are forbidden as footwear on Yom Kippur and Tishah B'Av. But this prohibition is contingent on the material from which the shoes are made.

The ingredient that renders shoes prohibited is leather. Shoes made from leather are forbidden. Shoes made from ingredients other than leather are not.

Running shoes can be leather free, in which case they are acceptable footwear for Yom Kippur and Tishah B'Av.

However, today, many running shoes, including the new and quite expensive models, are made with a significant amount of leather. No matter what amount of leather, running shoes that do contain that ingredient should not be worn on Yom Kippur and Tishah B'Av.

Misconception: Wishing someone, "Have an easy fast," is an appropriate greeting.

The sentiments in the greeting, "Have an easy fast," are quite commendable. They express the desire that the individual go through the protracted period of abstinence from food in a way that does not cause difficulty.

As much as the sentiment is commendable, the precise terminology is questionable. The purpose of a fast day is to be awakened to the meaning of the fast, to be agitated by the reasons for the fast, and to be inspired, through that agitation, to realize the fulfillment of the fast.

If the fast goes easily, this means that the individual has not fully comprehended its true meaning. It would be more appropriate to say, "Have a meaningful fast." This would incorporate all the concerns for the fast. After all, if the pangs of hunger were so excruciating, the discomfort would deny the individual the possibility for meaningfully fulfilling the purpose of the fast.

A meaningful fast incorporates physical and spiritual concerns; therefore, this wish is the more appropriate greeting.

Misconception: One for whom fasting is dangerous may still opt to do so.

Danger to life is a paramount consideration in Judaic practice. As a general rule, one is not permitted to place oneself in danger, even if it is for the purpose of fulfilling a command. It is preferable to be alive for the next day than to have the present fulfillment result in the preclusion of future fulfillment.

We must not ignore health and are prohibited from fasting if such fasting will create a life-threatening danger.

There are other ways in which the fast can be observed, including prayer, contemplation, and study, or, in the case of Yom Kippur, for example, genuine and complete repentance.

Fasting is just one component of the observance for that day. One who is forced to eat for health reasons should not look upon this as a negation of the entire day as a religious fulfillment.

Misconception: One who is exempt from observing a public fast may eat anything.

There are certain times in the year when the public is obliged to fast. These are the Fast of Gedalyah, Yom Kippur, the Fast of the Tenth of *Tevet*, the Fast of Esther, the Fast of the Seventeenth of *Tamuz*, and the Fast of Tishah B'Av.

However, certain individuals are exempt from fasting on those days. Primarily, people who would be endangered by fasting are permitted, and in fact obliged, to eat rather than endanger their lives.

Obviously, since Yom Kippur is a biblically mandated fast, the exemption from fasting on this day is not as readily forthcoming as it would be on other days. Tishah B'Av, because of its severity, is likewise in this category. When one is given permission to eat, it is for the purpose of avoiding any dangers that may accrue from fasting.

That being the case, the foods that should be eaten on these occasions should be primarily health-oriented foods. Luxury items such as ice cream and candy should be scrupulously avoided. One does not have carte blanche to eat everything.

The fast day remains a fast day even for those who are obliged to eat. Eating on Yom Kippur for health reasons does not exempt one from repenting on Yom Kippur.

One who is obliged for health reasons to eat on Tishah B'Av should nevertheless spend the balance of the time reading *Aykhah*, the Book of Lamentations, and focusing on the elegies, the *kinot*, that are basic to Tishah B'Av.

The fast day remains a day of contemplation whether or not one eats.

Misconception: There is no problem related to reciting the *Minhah* on the fast day, early in the afternoon.

On a fast day, those who fast recite a specific prayer of supplicatory nature in the *Amidah*. However, those who do not fast would not recite this addition to the *Amidah*.

Scheduling the afternoon service for early in the afternoon creates a possibly problematic scenario. This scenario would unfold if one intends to eat subsequent to the prayers and is praying early in order to eat immediately afterward.

This would retroactively engender the prayer recited during the fast as having been said in vain, because the individual actually had no intention of completing the fast.

It is best to set the *Minhah* time on a fast day for as close to sunset as possible. This avoids any possible problems because by the time *Minhah* is over, the fast is almost over.

11

Marriage

Misconception: There is no problem associated with a groom's having his *Aufruf* (call to the Torah prior to the wedding) two weeks before the wedding.

In many instances, because of distance, an *Aufruf* is scheduled for more than a few days before the wedding.

The wedding may be out of town or there may be other preparations in the way or other considerations that seemingly justify having an *Aufruf* much in advance of the wedding.

There is certainly nothing wrong with having an *Aliyah* (call to the Torah) at any time, but whether this can be legitimately called an *Aufruf* is questionable.

The idea of *Aufruf* is that a groom should be called to the Torah on the *Shabbat* of the week the wedding occurs. This is an *Aufruf* in its ideal form. It is intended to impress on the groom the notion that the wedding is not merely a social event. It is a spiritual experience, an uplifting call to embrace Torah ideals in married life.

In circumstances when, for whatever reason, it may be impossible to have a great celebration of this event on the *Shabbat* before the wedding, and therefore the celebratory event takes place a week or two before, a groom should make sure to be called to the Torah on the *Shabbat* before the wedding, even without a big splash afterward.

In the specific circumstance when a groom must travel to another city for the wedding and must leave prior to the *Shabbat* immediately preceding the wedding, the *Shabbat* before that is considered the *Aufruf Shabbat*.

That it is considered the *Aufruf Shabbat* gives the *hatan* (groom) the strongest claim for being called to the Torah. However, barring extenuating circumstances, one should endeavor to have the celebrative *Aufruf* on the *Shabbat* just before the wedding.

Misconception: There is no requirement for a groom to be called to the Torah on the *Shabbat* immediately after the wedding.

The *hatan* (groom), on the *Shabbat* immediately following the wedding, ranks high among the priority claims for being called to the Torah. His claim has priority even over one who is observing *Yahrzeit* (anniversary of the passing) for a parent.

This priority claim pertains only if the wedding took place in the latter part of the previous week, from Wednesday on.

But the importance of being called to the Torah applies no matter when the wedding took place the previous week. The new groom should be called to the Torah on the *Shabbat* immediately following the wedding. This means that he must be there, so as to set the marriage on a directed spiritual course linked with the Torah.

Misconception: It is forbidden for a woman to marry before her older sister.

General practice in Jewish families was for the older sister to marry first. The famous biblical episode in which Lavan tricked Yaakov into taking Leah, even though Yaakov's desire was to marry Rahel, was justified by Lavan with the explanation that it is not done in our place, that is, to give the younger daughter before the older daughter.

There is a logic in deferring to the older sister, but this is merely deference and a show of respect rather than legal stricture.

It would be folly for a family not to allow a younger sister to marry before an older sister finds the right mate. If perchance an older sister is having difficulty finding a mate, it is absurd to expand that difficulty by transmuting it into an entire family tragedy.

Deference, yes; straitjacket, no.

Misconception: There is no difficulty associated with a rabbi's charging a fee for officiating at a wedding.

Some rabbis, as a matter of principle, refuse to charge a fee for any service they may provide. They so refuse simply because they look upon the rabbinate as a calling and a responsibility, not a job.

On the other hand, there are rabbis who do charge for rabbinic services. Specifically there are rabbis who charge for officiating at weddings, funerals, and the like. Usually, congregational rabbis do not levy any fees. But in the reality of Jewish life today, there are many independent rabbis, unaffiliated with congregations, who are available for hire at the request of families who need them.

Rabbis who may be entirely unconnected to specific families may be called to officiate at weddings. Such rabbis invariably charge a fee for their services.

There are those who raise an objection to rabbis charging for performing a wedding ceremony. The objection inheres in a very simple consideration: the rabbi who charges a fee loses objectivity. He now has a vested interest in making sure that the marriage takes place because without that, he will not get the fee. He has something to gain from the marriage's being finalized and therefore can hardly be considered an objective party. To some, this compromises the rabbi's capacity to act as witness to the marriage, in the same way that relatives, who obviously have a vested interest, cannot be witnesses to the marriage.

Although the prevailing view is that such consideration does not disqualify a rabbi, it is by no means unanimous that the rabbi is not disqualified.

It is important to realize that a rabbi's charging of a fee does raise some legal problems. Perhaps it is most important for the rabbi, who would like to officiate in a manner devoid of all possible legal problems.

The rabbi is best advised not to charge anything for the marriage and to simply get a "charge" out of the knowledge that he has linked together a husband and wife in what it is hoped will be a viable and fulfilling union.

Misconception: There is no concern about placing a microphone under the *hupah* (wedding canopy) so that the audience can hear what transpires.

One of the essential components of the marriage ceremony is the recitation of the blessings. These blessings, most of them, must be recited in the presence of a *minyan* — and must be responded to by that quorum.

There is a view advanced by some that hearing this via a microphone is not sufficient, that it is secondhand and removed from immediacy, much like hearing the blessings recited via radio.

According to this view, blessings transmitted via a microphone and heard only by microphone are not considered heard by a *minyan*. Because most of these blessings may be recited only in the presence of a *minyan*, doing so via microphone may therefore be in the category of blessings recited in vain.

The only justification for using a microphone is if there are enough individuals in the vicinity of the *hupah* who can hear the blessings without benefit of the microphone, who hear the direct voice of those reciting the blessings. Otherwise, within this view, a microphone is a serious impediment to the viability of the marriage ceremony.

In the end, microphones have been accepted as standard for weddings, but it is important to be aware of the considerations that render microphone use problematic.

Misconception: There is no problem in using the mother's ring to finalize the *kiddushin* (betrothal).

The idea of betrothing one's bride with the mother's ring certainly has an attractive sentimentality. What better way of showing the interconnection of the generations! However, as much as sentimentality is important, and the interconnectedness of the generations is vital, there may be a serious problem associated with using the mother's ring.

If the mother has given the ring to the groom as a permanent gift, and therefore the groom now has the right to do with it as he pleases, it is not a problem. But usually, the mother lends the ring to the groom only for the purpose of using it under the *hupah* to effect the *kiddushin*. This is highly problematic. After all, the wedding ceremony is a legally binding action, cementing the relationship between the bride and the groom in a legal way.

It can hardly be viewed as legal if the groom gives the bride a ring the bride will have to return immediately afterward. There is much sentimentality, but very little permanence, in such a betrothal, and it should be avoided.

There may be legal ways of getting around this, for example, by buying the ring from the mother, but it is best that the ring the groom gives the bride under the *hupah* is the ring that will be the bride's forever.

Misconception: There is no objection to having a wedding on Sunday.

Although many people schedule weddings for Sunday, much concern, even objection, has been raised to this.

One concern is that having a wedding on Sunday may lead to desecration of the *Shabbat*. Some claim that this is an issue only if the wedding takes place immediately after *Shabbat*, on Saturday night, which according to Jewish calculation is already the first day of the week, although technically not yet Sunday.

Another concern is that Sunday weddings are an emulation of non-Jewish practice.

Sunday weddings are quite common, but there is no common awareness of the problems attached thereto. Sunday weddings are by now accepted practice, in spite of the enunciated concerns.

Misconception: There is no preferred day for a wedding.

One day that has been singled out as ideal for weddings is Tuesday, the day on which God saw that everything created was good, and the words "that it was good" are repeated twice. This has given to Tuesday a sense that it is a day for good.

Of course, there is nothing magical about this, and to rely on it can be dangerous. The main purpose behind this association is to use the biblical appellation for this day as a mood enhancer, to enter into the wedding with greater gusto, armed with the confidence projected in the biblical associations attached to that day.

Another day deemed ideal for weddings is Wednesday (or at night on Tuesday, which is by then the fourth day of the week), because that day is linked to blessing and also because those who are some distance away can come before *Shabbat* and return before *Shabbat*.

The fifth day (Thursday, but really already at night on Wednesday) is considered specially fitting for a wedding because a blessing for fruitfulness was given on the fifth day of creation.

The added advantage to marrying on these days is that a weekday wedding is usually less expensive than on the weekend.

Misconception: One must have a *minyan* for a wedding.

It is highly preferable to have a *minyan* when uniting a man and a woman in matrimony. However, this may not always be possible.

The basic essentials that are necessary for a wedding, in terms of people present, are a bride, a groom, and two witnesses. One of the witnesses may be the officiating rabbi, so that when a fifth person is not available, the wedding can proceed.

In other words, a bride and groom and two witnesses, one of whom is the officiating rabbi, suffice for a wedding.

Such a wedding, though a last resort, is valid and legally binding.

Misconception: A wedding without a *minyan* is no different from a wedding with a quorum present.

Although a wedding can take place with a minimum of four people, the presence of a *minyan* is most desirable.

One of the main reasons for this is that in the absence of a *minyan*, one may not recite the seven blessings that are basic to the wedding ceremony.

In the absence of a *minyan*, only the first blessing — over wine — and the final blessing of the seven may be recited. Regarding the seventh blessing, there is actually some halakhic debate as to whether it can be recited in the absence of a *minyan*. At the very least, three people must be present for this blessing to be recited.

The seventh blessing ends with the culminating words describing God as the One who gladdens the bride and groom. The godly ingredient in the wedding is basic and indispensable. Reference to it can be made even in the absence of a *minyan*. But the full complement of blessings demands the presence of a *minyan*.

A wedding with or without a *minyan* is valid, but the marriage that takes place in the presence of a *minyan* is different.

Misconception: There are no lingering consequences for having a wedding without a *minyan*.

It is vitally important that a *minyan* be present and attentive at a wedding.

However, there are extenuating circumstances when it is simply not possible to gather a *minyan* for the wedding. The wedding proceeds but without the all-important *Sheva Berakhot*.

These blessings are so important to the marriage that they must be recited at the first opportunity the bride and groom have to gather a *minyan* or to go and be in the presence of a *minyan*.

Every marriage is in need of blessing.

Misconception: For the week after the wedding, one may recite the *Sheva Berakhot* only once a day.

It is the proper practice, during the week following the wedding, including the actual day of the wedding, to recite the Seven Blessings at gatherings that are called *Sheva Berakhot*. These gatherings, festive meals, adopt the name that refers to the blessings, which are recited at these meals.

On any occasion that is called specifically for the purpose of celebrating with the new bride and groom and on which a quorum of ten, a *minyan*, is present, the *Sheva Berakhot* should be recited.

If such occasions with a quorum present actually unfold at breakfast, lunch, and supper, these *Sheva Berakhot* should be recited at all these occasions.

The key components are that it be a meal purposely arranged to gladden the bride and groom, that there be a *minyan* present, that the bride and groom be there, and that a new face be among those who constitute the quorum.

Misconception: The obligation to love your neighbor does not relate to married life.

The obligation to love your neighbor is probably most difficult to achieve and highly problematic to understand.

If the Torah urges that we love our neighbor as we love ourself, this would mean that we are obliged to take care of our neighbors' needs before we take care of our own, or at least simultaneous with taking care of our own. Thus, the whole neighborhood should be eating breakfast, lunch, and supper with us; the entire neighborhood's needs should be taken care of simultaneous with our needs. It is immediately obvious that such an ideal is impossible to achieve. Its impossibility resides in its overwhelmingness.

The Torah does not ask of us the impossible, so it is important to understand what exactly is meant by the obligation to love your neighbor, literally to love your *re'ah*.

Re'ah is a term that is used to refer to one's mate, one's spouse. It is therefore consistent with the talmudic understanding of this verse, and the understanding of many commentaries, that this is a biblical obligation asking us to love our spouse as we love ourself.

Asking that we take care of the needs of our spouse simultaneous with our own needs is not only possible but also eminently desirable. It is the formula that guarantees the fulfillments that are forthcoming in a harmonious marriage.

Misconception: A woman may go to the *mikvah* only after seven complete days have elapsed since the cessation of her menstrual flow.

This is usually the rule, but it is a rule that does have an exception. If the woman in question should complete her seven days on a Friday night, then under certain circumstances it is possible for her to go to the *mikvah* for ritual immersion prior to the completion of the seven days.

If the completion of the seven days comes on a Friday night, this would necessitate her going to the *mikvah* on the *Shabbat*, which in itself is not a problem. However, it may become a problem if following that, the woman cannot get back to her home because the distance between the *mikvah* and the home is too great or because the path from the *mikvah* to the home is fraught with danger.

In these instances, allowance is made for the woman to immerse herself in the *mikvah* as close to *Shabbat* as possible, with enough time for her to return home before the kindling of the *Shabbat* lights.

When such license is enlisted, the husband should vacate the house prior to the wife's return home, so that they are not together, alone, until after the completion of the full seven days. He should make sure not to return from the *Bet Knesset* until after dark.

This is a flexibility that expresses the strong desire that husband and wife should not be separated unnecessarily, even if it is for one extra day, because of the wife's inability to go to the *mikvah* on Friday night proper. Husband-wife togetherness is too vital, and therefore such allowance is granted within the framework of Jewish law.

Misconception: The idea that one should not directly ask one's spouse to engage in conjugal union is prudish.

This idea may seem prudish, based on the notion of openness and unabashedness that reigns supreme in modern times. However, Jewish law accentuates the importance of modesty in everything we do and certainly in something as delicate as marital relations.

Marital relations should not work on a demand basis. They must always work on a mutuality basis. Failing that, the likelihood of abuse is significantly increased, and the attendant affliction is unconscionable.

Direct asking is not advisable for other, more practical reasons as well. The spouse to whom the request is extended is now under pressure to perform, rather than spontaneously expressing emotional attachment. Such a natural relationship must evolve spontaneously and naturally, rather than artificially.

In addition, if the other partner is not in the mood and responds negatively, this may create a downward spiral, starting with the unfortunate and unnecessary feeling on the part of the asking spouse that he or she has been rejected.

This is no more the case than is the absurd conclusion that because one does not want to eat an offered meal, one is rejecting the other person and the person's culinary skills. The person may simply not be hungry. But in the delicacy of the relationship, a "no" may be misinterpreted, however irrational such misinterpretation may be.

It is for reasons of modesty and eminent logic, therefore, that it is always best not to directly ask for conjugal consummation but rather to have the act evolve in the natural flow of the marital dynamic.

Misconception: The rules of modesty apply only to women.

The rules of modesty relating to women are well known. But it is a gross misperception to think that the rules of modesty apply to women only. The idea of being modest is a notion that applies to both men and women.

Men are enjoined from parading in the nude, even if it is in the privacy of their own room when they are alone. They are urged to dress in a way that their most private parts are not exposed, again even if they are alone and no one else can see. How much more so is this the case in a public area, such as a locker room in a health club.

Modesty is considered one of the most important ingredients for an individual's attainment of a sense of the godly, and attaining a sense of the Godly is the task of both men and women.

Misconception: The *ketubah* (marriage contract) is the prime protection for women in marriage.

The *ketubah* is definitely a protection for women in marriage. It guarantees a wife a financial settlement following divorce, so a husband will think very carefully before exiting from the marriage. The knowledge that there are financial consequences to such exit acts as a form of protection against irrational behavior.

However, a woman has an even more potent protection. The most effective check against a husband's precipitously throwing the divorce into his wife's face is the edict of Rabbenu Gershom, which prevents a husband from divorcing his wife against her will. The divorce can be finalized only with a wife's agreement.

This represents a more potent check on divorce than even the *ketubah* does. The *ketubah* itself usually calls for a settlement in the neighborhood of two hundred *zuzim* which is not a great sum, and in most instances would not present such a great obstacle in the path of an irresponsible husband. But the knowledge that a divorce cannot be finalized without a wife's agreement acts as a powerful check against a husband's irresponsible behavior.

Misconception: It is not that serious if a wife has lost her *ketubah*.

It would not seem to be such an important matter if the *ketubah* is lost, since the couple are married anyway. However, the *ketubah* was instituted by the rabbis as a form of marital insurance policy so that a husband should never think that divorcing his wife is a simple matter. The *ketubah* settlement that is guaranteed to the wife acts as a check against the husband's wielding the divorce stick.

In the post–Rabbenu Gershom era, when women have the added protection of the inability of a husband to divorce his wife against her will, the *ketubah* document is obviously not as necessary a check against indiscriminate divorce.

However, it is still a vital component of the marital compact. If a wife should lose her *ketubah*, she should immediately go to her rabbi (when possible, the rabbi who finalized the marriage) and arrange for a replacement *ketubah* to be written and signed. This is easily done, and it is important that it be done as soon as possible.

12

Divorce

Misconception: Jewish family life in talmudic times was smooth and harmonious.

There is certainly much written in the Talmud about the importance of family harmony. Specifically, the Talmud calls upon the husband to honor his wife more than himself. The rabbis argue that a man's blessing in his home can come only from his wife.

There was thus a great recognition of the importance of harmony and of the specific role the husband played in effecting that harmony. However, there is evidence that such harmony did not always prevail. The Talmud mentions that abstinence vows made out of anger were not a rare occurrence. Obviously, in a situation of harmony, abstinence vows are not a normative expression.

Our ancestors had difficulties, which were addressed, and complications, which had to be confronted.

In a contemplation of the preponderance of divorce in today's society, it is wrong to presume that this is the first generation in which marital problems exist. We may have a higher divorce rate, but this does not mean we have a higher unhappiness rate.

Maybe some measure of the persistence capacities of our forebears would help us wade through the sometimes swampy marital waters.

Misconception: Jews have always had a low divorce rate.

In previous generations, the Jewish rate of divorce was significantly higher than in society at large. This does not mean that Jews were more unhappy. Possibly, it means only that they had an escape from unhappiness. Within Jewish life, divorce was always possible. Divorce had already been spelled out as a contingency in the Torah itself. Divorce was obviously not encouraged, but its possibility remained intact. There is evidence that in previous generations there was a significant rate of divorce in certain places within the Jewish community.

The Jewish family has long stood out as a model of family life. The Jewish marriage ideal has long been espoused as essential to Jewish continuity. This remains as true today as it was in yesteryear.

But one should not live with the delusion that all was harmonious in the Jewish home of yesteryear. This may have been the general rule, but certainly there were many exceptions to that rule.

Misconception: A divorced woman who has not married a second mate may always remarry her first husband.

Under normal circumstances, a woman who has been divorced from her husband may remarry him, provided she has not married someone else in the interim.

However, this is not always the case. There are times when the divorced woman may not remarry her original husband. If her husband is a *Kohen*, she may not remarry him, since that *Kohen* may not marry a divorced woman.

In addition, if the original divorce was because of the wife's infidelity, then at no time may the wife remarry her husband.

Misconception: The granting of a *get* (Jewish divorce) is not a *mitzvah*.

The most important *mitzvah* in the husband's and wife's getting together is for each to enhance the other, to effect harmony between them, and to encourage mutual growth in their shared destiny together.

When a marriage has not worked out, the couple do not simply say good-bye to each other and part company. Marriage is sacred at both ends—at its beginning and at its terminus. In the same way a sacred act governs the initiation of the relationship, so does a sacred act govern the termination of that relationship.

That sacred procedure, a *havdalah* (separation) of sorts, is known as a *get*. *Get* is the sacred process of unbinding the couple who had been bound together in marriage.

It is a *mitzvah*, an affirmative obligation, to effect this divorce, this parting of the ways, through this religious act.

The granting of a *get* is a conditional *mitzvah* affirmation in that this obligation becomes operative only if and when the marriage has been so ruptured that repair is impossible and divorce is the only option.

Misconception: There is no specific Jewish divorce ethic.

Divorce is not one of the pleasant experiences of life, and presumably it was not very prevalent in Jewish life, at least until recently, so there is much that is not known about the Jewish approach to divorce.

One of the unknowns is the ethics of divorce. There is an ethical way to divorce, as indeed there is an ethical way to engage in any human activity. Love and union have an ethic of their own; separation and divorce have an ethic of their own.

In general terms, the ethic of separation and divorce calls upon the separating partners to do so with the minimum of pain and with the elimination of hate-infused behavior toward each other. Obviously, this sounds slightly difficult, to say the least. After all, if the couple were on such friendly terms, they would stay together. However, ethics never is easy, because human beings do not readily feel like going out of their way, controlling their emotions, or stifling their feelings. A general code of ethics exists precisely because there is a tendency to be anything but ethical and decent.

Once a couple decides to divorce, they should realize they are out of the pressure cooker wherein they must love each other. They are now in a different situation in which love is obviously out of question. But that love need not be replaced by hate.

In the absence of love, and in the dissolving of the union, the previous unharmonious situation is best replaced by a modicum of civility and respect from a distance. As difficult as this may seem, and as unrealistic as it may appear, it is possible, it is achievable, and most important, from the point of view of the couple and their offspring, it is eminently desirable.

Misconception: For a divorcing couple, the *get* should be finalized only after the granting of the civil divorce.

In Israel, the religious divorce and the civil divorce are one and the same. One may go to a rabbinic court and have all the outstanding issues in the divorce addressed, including support, custody, and the legally recognized divorce. Outside Israel, of course, this is not the case.

Outside Israel, we are governed by the laws of the state. Certainly, no one should contemplate remarrying with only a Jewish divorce in hand. The law requires a civil divorce, and only following that should a new marriage be finalized. This is obviously on the proviso that a *get* has also been obtained.

However, the *get* procedure is effectively independent of the civil divorce. Both are necessary, but there is no reason one should delay the finalization of the *get* by waiting for it until the civil divorce has come through.

The argument is precisely the reverse. Once it has become clear that the marriage is doomed and divorce unavoidable, the *get* should be finalized immediately.

Misconception: A husband can forgive his wife's adultery and maintain the marriage.

In Jewish law, adultery is the most serious breach of the marital compact. It violates the fundamental foundation of the marriage.

The marital union is a sacred union. The sanctity of that union is expressed in many ways, but none is more fundamental than that the husband and wife are as one, united in body and soul.

Once that unity has been compromised through the wife's adultery, the marriage has reached the point of no return. It is not within the power of the husband to forgive. Jewish law allows for the repair of all damage within marriage, except for the one damage that is irreparable, namely, adultery.

However, it should be clear that such adultery is not construed to have taken place just by the wife's having gone somewhere with someone else. Even the wife's admitting that she has had an affair with someone may be only a ruse to anger the husband or to shock him into taking more notice of her.

The adultery that signals the rupture of a marriage is one that is based on fact, on eyewitness testimony, rather than on allegation or even personal admission.

Misconception: A husband's adultery is not grounds for divorce.

According to Torah law, in ancient times a husband was allowed to have many wives. This would suggest that a husband's having an affair with another woman may not necessarily pose a difficulty in marriage. After all, a husband may argue, "Biblically I could legally have more than one wife, so why should it bother my wife if I had an extramarital affair?"

But this is not the case. The only difference between a wife's adultery and a husband's adultery is that when a wife commits adultery, the breach cannot be repaired. When a husband commits adultery, it is within a wife's power to forgive. However, it also is eminently within a wife's power to refuse to forgive, considering this an unpardonable trespass and violation of the marriage.

She would certainly be within her rights to demand a divorce. This would be supported by the rabbinical court, and she would be granted the divorce with the full marital settlement to which she is entitled.

Misconception: That the wife finds her husband repulsive is not grounds for divorce.

Being repulsive is often a subjective feeling. Some people may find the behavior of others repulsive, while others may not mind that behavior and are able to persevere.

A wife whose husband is an incorrigible slob or has an offensive odor should obviously try to have her husband correct these manifestations.

However, if all these efforts are in vain, and a husband insists on maintaining the slobbishness or the malodorous emanation, a wife is within her full rights to demand a divorce.

Jewish law cannot justify imposing upon a woman that she has to endure the agony and torment of being in the company of someone who repulses her.

268

Misconception: A woman who knew before marriage that her husband-to-be works in a tannery and who now cannot tolerate the smell cannot demand a divorce.

It would seem that a man who makes his living in a tannery and warns his wife-to-be before marriage that this is the case has adequately covered his bases.

After all, he has warned her about where her bread will be coming from, and she has readily accepted this.

He may even have given the wife-to-be some smell of what she should anticipate in the marriage. However, all this is irrelevant.

If, after marriage, the previously understanding and accepting wife finds that she cannot abide the smell from the tannery, and the husband has no other source of income and must continue in the tannery, then obviously something must give.

The previously accepting wife who now says that it is impossible to live with this smell may sue for divorce on the grounds that she finds life with this stench unbearable.

Misconception: It is perfectly acceptable to go through a secular court to finalize the details of a divorce settlement.

This presumption has certainly gained much currency in our generation. We would not dream of finalizing a marriage through the secular court, but when it comes to divorce, this seems to be a different matter.

There is some reason for this anomaly. It is that the rabbinic court does not have the power to make the final arrangements. This is a power that is given to, or taken by, the state.

Even the power to effect a marriage in a secular society is a power invested in the rabbi by the secular state. It is only because of that recognition that the marriage is valid in civil law.

But unlike previous generations, and certainly unlike what pertains in Israel, civil divorce is the rule. If the rabbis imposed a divorce settlement, this could be contested in court, and the court would go by its own protocol in imposing a divorce settlement.

However, this does not mean that this is the ideal. There are great problems involved in going to a secular court. The secular court may have different ways of splitting assets or of granting custody.

There are grave questions involved in this, especially if the civil court adjudication were to run contrary to Jewish law. In this instance, the party eliciting greater amounts through the civil court may be guilty of taking money from others in an illegal fashion.

Couples who are divorcing are best off seeking rabbinic arbitration of their cases. If they agree to this arbitration, the rabbis will weigh the merits of the claims, come up with a financial settlement to satisfy both sides as best as possible, and arrange custody in a way that reflects the best interests of the child or children.

A couple agreeing to this goes a long way toward avoiding legal hassles. The lawyers who incorporate this rabbinic solution will usually find very little opposition from an already overloaded court system, which greatly welcomes outside help of this sort.

Since the rabbinic solution is consistent with the Jewish law regarding divorce, a rabbinic court is the appropriate place to adjudicate divorces.

Misconception: No-fault divorce has never been part of Jewish divorce procedure.

In Jewish law, there is a long list of grounds for divorce for both the husband and wife, who are entitled to pursue divorce if a marital partner fails to comply with the halakhic protocols of marriage.

However, there are occasions when divorce may not be precipitated by infidelity, abuse, or neglect of fiscal responsibility. It may just be that the husband and wife, try as they may, have not been able to harmonize.

It is no one's fault. Each one realizes that the marriage is not working. After everything they may try, they realize the futility of their union and mutually decide to part as friends and to seek their fulfillment elsewhere.

In a situation when husband and wife agree that divorce is their only alternative, but they have no serious accusation to hurl against each other, Jewish law still permits divorce. This reality is a fundamental component of Jewish law regarding divorce. It predates the more modern discovery of no-fault divorce.

The idea that husband and wife may divorce without any grounds may be new to today's generation, but it is certainly not new to Jewish law. Jewish law never sought to impose upon people that they must stay together even though unhappy. This has never been the Jewish way.

Misconception: It is permissible to counter lies with lies in order to get a better divorce settlement.

In the heat of the postseparation argumentation that goes on between husband and wife, matters sometimes seem to be carried way out of proportion.

One of the spouses is likely to exaggerate either the other's offenses or their own needs or their own qualifications, whatever the case may be.

It is a great temptation to counter one exaggeration with another so as to neutralize the lies of one side with lies by the other side.

However, no amount of lying by any individual justifies lying by others. For example, a husband who has been wrongly accused of neglecting the children by never being home cannot counter with his own lie, say, that his wife abuses the children.

The obligation of individuals to tell the truth and to adhere to the truth is not contingent on other people also telling the truth. An unconditional and unswerving commitment to honesty prevails at all times.

Misconception: After finalization of the divorce settlement, the ex-husband has no financial obligations toward his ex-wife.

The finalization of the divorce settlement usually brings with it some form of recompense from husband to wife.

From a civil point of view, it would seem that once a settlement has been reached, the ex-husband has no more financial obligation toward his ex-wife. Legally, this is probably true. But obligations go beyond legalities. For example, no one has a legal obligation to the poor, at least not in the sense that the poor can demand money from those who have it. There is a biblical obligation of all individuals to share their money in a charitable fashion, but no one has a claim on it. It is a claim that belongs in the public domain.

However, a husband who has divorced his wife has a special obligation to her that prevails even after divorce. It is in the nature of the prophetic charge not to be oblivious to your own flesh, that is, to the one who previously had been as your flesh—your marital partner. An ex-husband who sees his ex-wife wallowing in poverty and who can rescue her from that poverty must do so. This is not a legal imposition, actionable in court. It is a moral obligation that rests on the ex-husband for as long as his ex-wife is his ex-wife, which is forever.

One way or another, the marriage and the implications of the marriage endure.

Misconception: There is no record of custody conflict in the Bible.

The famous episode of the contending mothers who argued their cases before Shlomoh HaMelekh (King Solomon) was in effect a conflict over custody. It was not between a divorcing husband and wife, but it was a bitter conflict.

Each of the mothers had given birth, but one's baby died. Each mother claimed that the surviving child was hers. The wise king, unable to judge which mother was telling the truth, ordered the baby cut in half and split between the mothers.

One of the protagonists thought this a "fair" way out of the quarrel. The other rejected the solution, offering that she would waive her claim and allow the other woman to raise the child, as long as the child would not be cut in half.

Upon hearing this, Shlomoh HaMelekh immediately declared that the child be given to the woman who refused to allow the baby to be cut in half.

That woman may not have been the biological mother, but she was the truly fit mother and thus was granted custody.

Misconception: In Jewish law, the mother always gains custody following divorce.

In general, in Jewish law, the custody of a child is decided by certain principles. The first principle is that the mother is usually granted custody of all children who are younger than six years of age. However, this custody is not granted permanently. It is granted until the time the children attain the age of six years. After that, the general norm for custody is that boys go to their fathers and girls remain with their mothers.

This is the general principle. However, the rabbinic court, which has been entrusted with making the custody recommendations, will always base its final adjudication on what it perceives to be in the best interests of the child.

There are times when it is better for a boy to be with his mother; there are times when it is better for a girl to be with her father. All depends on the individual circumstance.

Even if a child is younger than six, when the norm is that the child goes to the mother, this may not always be the case. For instance, an alcoholic mother may be denied custody, as would a violent and temperamental mother who beats her children. This may be an unusual circumstance, but unfortunately the unusual sometimes occurs.

Thus, there are significant exceptions to the rule that the mother always gains custody following divorce.

Misconception: The agreement of divorcing parents on custody is automatically accepted by the rabbinic court.

When a *Bet Din* (rabbinic court) is entrusted with the responsibility for adjudicating custody, as is often the case in Israel, the parental agreement on custodial arrangements is obviously a welcome prospect. It usually shows a sense of cooperation, a sense of fair play, and compromise, and it bodes well for the future.

As such, the rabbinic court is likely to look favorably upon such an agreement and also upon the spirit with which it was achieved. However, this does not mean that such an agreement is automatically accepted. For example, the couple may have come to some form of custodial arrangement on the basis of a trade-off. The wife may have granted custody to the husband in exchange for a more generous monetary settlement. But this arrangement may not be in the best interests of the children, who may very much need their mother.

There are other such scenarios wherein the custodial arrangement agreed to by the parents may not be in the best interests of the children. In those instances, the *Bet Din* has the right, and the responsibility, to reject such an arrangement and to provide an alternative, which will be in the best interests of the children.

Misconception: A visitation to the child is a parental right.

The statement that visitation to a child is a parental right may reflect the legal niceties of secular vintage.

However, in Jewish law, child visitation is not a parental right; it is a parental responsibility. It is the responsibility of a parent to take care of children and, following divorce, to retain contact with the children and therefore give them the spiritual sustenance and nourishment they need.

However, because the nature of the relationship emanates from parental responsibility, a parent cannot demand to visit a child. It is a child's right to refuse such visitation. It is also the court's right and responsibility to disallow such visitation, if the rabbinic court feels such visitation is harmful to the child.

Certainly, a parent who physically or verbally abuses a child distorts the nature of the parent-child relationship. Such a parent cannot impose upon the child and would thus be denied visitation if it were so obviously harmful.

Misconception: A child has no say about which of the parents gains custody following divorce.

The operative principle insofar as custody is concerned is that the rabbinic court entrusted with adjudicating custody arrangements looks out for the best interests of the child. What are the best interests of the child? This is often a very difficult question, and it is not always a certainty that the answer given is the correct one.

In the deliberations that take place to most accurately decide upon the best course for the custodial arrangements, the court must weigh various considerations. Obviously, it will examine the personalities and behavior patterns of the parents and the level of emotional support the child or children can expect from them.

The court will also try to gauge the nature of the parent-child relationship from the perspective of the child. Although very often the child is a pawn in the verbal fisticuffs that prevail between husband and wife, the rabbinic tribunal will try to glean an objective assessment from the child.

A child who spontaneously, without being rehearsed, states a very clear preference based, for example, on maltreatment by one of the parents, will make a definite impact on the rabbinic tribunal. The child's testimony, if genuine and sincere, may often be the key component in the rabbinic court decision as to who would be the better custodial parent.

13

Parents and Children

Misconception: A child born out of wedlock is a *mamzer* (nonlegitimate).

To the secular mind, and based on general law, any child born out of wedlock is considered illegitimate. However, this was never the Judaic definition of *mamzer*. In Jewish law, one is a *mamzer* only if one's birth is the result of a specific type of prohibited relationship. For example, a child born out of a relationship between a brother and sister, a father and daughter, or a mother and son would in each case be a *mamzer*. These are instances wherein the consanguineous nature of the relationship confers illegitimacy both on the relationship and on its fruits.

Another type of nonlegitimate relationship that effects illegitimacy is that between a man of any marital status and a woman who is already married. In that type of circumstance, the child born of such an adulterous relationship is considered a *mamzer*. However, a child born out of wedlock, that is, born of a relationship between two unmarried individuals, is not a *mamzer*.

This is not to suggest that such a relationship is legitimized. It is only to suggest that the prohibition associated with out-of-wedlock relationships is not nearly as severe as that associated with adulterous or consanguineous relationships and therefore does not confer illegitimacy upon the child.

Misconception: The notion of *mamzer* punishes a child for the sin of its parents.

An illegitimate child, what is referred to in the Torah as a *mamzer*, is severely restricted in terms of marital possibilities.

A *mamzer* cannot marry within the normative community. This is a severe restriction. At first glance, this is a classic instance of children's suffering from the misbehavior of the parents. Although it is probably folly to argue differently, because this is a fact, it should be clear that this is not the intention.

The purpose of the entire institution of nonlegitimacy is to impress upon adults who are contemplating adultery that the consequences of that action are long lasting and painful. Unfortunately, only the notion that the pain lingers forever can push home this point.

As with other punitive measures in the Torah, it is the firm hope that the consequences of an illicit action will prevent the illicit activity.

It should be noted that a *mamzer* who developed into a sage was highly respected within the community. Such an individual was not restricted in terms of making an impact on the community.

Certainly, it seems unfair to blame a *mamzer* for the sins of the would-be father and mother. But the potential parents, knowing full well that the momentary pleasure will result in permanent consequence, will, it is hoped, have enough sense to control their passions.

Misconception: "One who spares the rod spoils the child" is the correct translation of that famous proverb.

Absolutely not. The precise translation of the proverb reads as follows: "One who holds back the rod hates the child."

There is a world of difference between the two translations. The first translation, "One who spares the rod spoils the child," suggests that it is imperative to hit the child. Failure to hit the child will cause the child to become spoiled. It is almost as if child-beating becomes a pedagogical imperative in this faulty translation.

The correct translation merely states that holding back the rod shows that the parent hates the child. Holding back the rod means the parent is not concerned enough to impose discipline and eliminates the rod as a contingency.

It is best if the rod is never necessary. But if you really love your child, your primary desire will be to make sure the child goes on the upright moral and ethical path.

In children's early stages, it may be that the only language they understand is the language of authority. The authority need not be used, but sometimes the threat of its being used can make a positive impact on children.

A parent who has no desire to insist on the child's proper behavior—what is implied in the idea of putting away the rod—shows disdain for the child's development. This is hate rather than love.

A parent who loves is a parent who is concerned. A parent who shows no concern and who could not care less about the child's behavior in effect is showing that hatred of the child.

A parent may deny hating the child by insisting he or she does not want to do anything to hurt the child by hitting. But if a parent is lackadaisical about a child's development, the result may be that the child is more likely to grow up delinquent.

Is there any greater manifestation of hate than for parents to allow this to happen?

Misconception: We are obligated to fear our parents.

One standard translation of the biblical verse regarding this relationship between fear and parents states, " . . . Fear your mother and father . . ." However, that translation is not precise. The word that is usually translated as "fear" really refers to awe. We are obliged to be in awe of our parents. Awe refers to positive, healthy respect.

Fear can never be the basis of an authentic and meaningful relationship. Fear is an instrumentality that drives a wedge between people and creates emotional distance even as it imposes physical proximity.

We should not fear parents any more than we should fear God. We should be in awe of our parents, as indeed we should be in awe of God. But awe is an ingredient that affects a relationship positively. It inspires upward.

Misconception: Children are punished for the sins of their parents.

Parental misdemeanor may adversely affect a child who is therefore being educated in a less-than-ideal home environment and is being given a poor model to emulate.

The Torah mention that God remembers the sins of the parent for four generations does not necessarily mean that God punishes the children. It suggests that God remembers and therefore understands the deviance of the child and is more tolerant because of the awareness that this is not the child's fault.

Generally, the most crucial principle in Jewish thinking is that children do not die for the sins of their parents; nor do parents die for the sins of their children.

If children are punished for the evils of their parents, it is nothing more or less than the natural and unfortunate consequences of living in a perverse environment. In such instance the child, although a victim, is certainly not blamed.

Misconception: All children have an equal obligation to care for their parents in the later years.

The obligation to care for parents in later years is directly related to the amount of time available to the children. Time availability is also associated with freedom of movement and the capacity to extend care in a direct manner.

A woman who marries has under normal circumstances undertaken a singular responsibility toward the family that she is marrying into, toward the husband, and toward future children. As such, it is unfair to place upon the woman the additional, onerous burden of having to take care of the parents. Superimposing this upon the already significant burden of caring for the family constitutes too great a responsibility.

Conversely, husbands have much more freedom because family responsibilities usually rest with women. Therefore, the primary responsibility for taking care of parents falls upon sons.

However, all of this is dependent on the situation of the specific family. Thus, for example, a woman who has divorced may thereby become free from her family responsibilities. She would share equally in the obligation to care for the parents, provided that in her single state, she is not doubly burdened with caring for the house and earning a livelihood.

In addition, a woman who has much more freedom in the marriage also shares more equal responsibility to care for the parents. For example, a woman has the full right to insist to her husband that she does not want to be burdened with the primary household responsibilities. In the trade, the husband is relieved of direct financial responsibility for her, but the option is always the woman's.

In this instance, it is clear that the woman has the same fundamental responsibilities in the marriage situation as the man and therefore has equal responsibility to care for the parents—equal, that is, to her brother or brothers, who are presumably free enough to address these sacred responsibilities.

No matter what the relationship of the siblings in their specific marriages, it is generally the case, with some exceptions, that daughters are much more sensitive and caring toward their parents than are sons. It may not be that they care more but that they show it more. This is the case even if they are burdened with the full complement of marital responsibilities.

Thus, even though the law lets women off the hook, they refuse to be unhooked from that responsibility.

Misconception: There is no problem associated with writing a will.

The Torah describes the basic components of the transmission of an estate from parent to child or children following a parent's demise. Children have priority over others, and the firstborn is allotted a portion double that of the other children.

This is a biblical mandate. One who writes a will that is inconsistent with this biblical mandate contravenes a Torah law and renders the will null and void from a Torah point of view. The fact that a court of law will uphold it is a fact of life but does not change the Jewish law that requires a specific way of apportioning.

A person who decides to disinherit the children and give the estate to others may feel fully empowered to do so but in Jewish law has no such right. On the other hand, this does not mean there is no Judaic legal recourse that incorporates the Torah formula but does not tie down the parents.

Parents may give away any part of their estate while still alive. This opens up another possibility insofar as the will is concerned. The parent may write not a will but a transmission of a gift, that gift to take effect five minutes before the parent passes on. It is not a will in the classic sense because it is not the transmission of an estate from a deceased person to survivors. It rather becomes the gift given to other individuals by an almost dead person. Anyone has a right to do this as long as one is alive.

Misconception: If a parent requested to be cremated, the child must obey that request.

As a general rule, children are obliged to adhere to the requests of their parents. There is also a general obligation to fulfill the expressed desires of one who has died. If the deceased is a parent, adherence to parental wishes becomes a potent double imperative. However, this applies only to a parental wish that is consistent with Jewish law. Cremation is not consistent with Jewish law.

Jewish law insists that except for specific life-threatening (as in cases of a plague) or life-preserving (as in transplantation) circumstances, an individual who dies must be buried by being returned in full to the earth. Therefore, a parental request to be cremated must be rejected. It would be advisable for parents contemplating cremation to be aware that their request will be rejected, or at least should be rejected, by their children.

It is hoped that with the knowledge that such a request will be rejected, and in fact must be rejected, parents will cease to make this request, which places the children in such an uncomfortable position.

Misconception: There is no *mitzvah* involved in kissing one's grandparent.

It is true that there is no explicit statement in the Bible asking individuals to kiss their grandparents. As a matter of fact, there is no statement in the Bible calling upon individuals to kiss their parents.

However, we are obligated to honor our parents. There is no greater way to show how our parents are genuinely honored than to show they are appreciated, acknowledged, and even loved. A sincere kiss is a prime manifestation of this love and honor.

We are additionally obliged to honor our grandparents, who are, after all, the parents of our own parents. If honor is shown to parents through a genuine kiss, it stands to reason that the same would apply to a grandparent.

By kissing grandparents, we show they are honored — we honor and appreciate them.

This is a *mitzvah* par excellence.

14

New Homes, New Children

Misconception: That Tuesday is the preferred day for moving is a superstition.

Tuesday is the preferred day for moving, but there is nothing magical about moving to a new home on Tuesday. Moving on Tuesday does not guarantee that the landlord will lower the rent or that the house will be impervious to any damage, whether by flood, gas leakage, fire, or whatever.

Moving on Tuesday is related to the fact that in the Torah, the words "that it was good" are mentioned twice on the Tuesday. We move on Tuesday to associate our life rhythm with the biblical verse.

This is not a magical incantation; it is rather a meaningful association with the text that means the most in our life. It is to create a linkage that we hope will envelop the house, so that the home abides by Torah rules and practices throughout the time of one's stay in that abode.

Misconception: There is no blessing recited upon buying a house.

Buying a house, building a house, even rebuilding a house that has been destroyed by a fire, tornado, or earthquake is a meaningfully joyous event. Upon its purchase or completion, one recites the *Sheheheyanu* blessing, extolling God, who has sustained the new homeowner to relish this great time.

Buying or building a house is a religious construct.

Misconception: In naming a child after someone, the key is that the name should sound the same.

Sometimes, parents feel uncomfortable giving an individual exactly the same name as the deceased relative one desires to honor. This may be the case when the original is a Yiddish name, which is not so desirable in contemporary times.

There may also be other factors involved that make it difficult to bestow the exact name. This happens most often when the child who is born is the opposite sex from the person for whom the child is being named.

The key to selection of a name is not to give a name with the same sound or even with the same first letter. The key is to select a name that has the same meaning as the name of the deceased whom one desires to honor. For instance, in naming a girl after someone who was Shlomoh, it would be wrong to give a name such as Shaynah just because the name starts with the same "sh" sound. However, giving a name such as Shulamit, which has the same basic meaning as Shlomoh, connoting peace, would be highly appropriate. And in this instance, the name Shulamit actually has the same first letter; in fact, even the first three Hebrew letters.

Alternatively, if the deceased person whom one wants to memorialize was named Frayda, one should not automatically give a name such as Fischel, which has the same first letter. A name such as Simhah relates more to Frayda and would be much more appropriate, because both Simhah and Frayda mean joy and happiness.

Misconception: In naming a child after someone, one must be sure that both the Jewish and secular names relate to the person for whom the child is being named.

When naming after someone, one should be aware that the key ingredient is the Jewish name. The secular name is for all practical purposes irrelevant. As a matter of fact, it is highly questionable whether secular names should be given altogether, because this is a throwback to exile times and certainly was not Jewish practice prior to that.

We remain one of the few ethnic groups that give two sets of names, and that only outside Israel. In Israel, Jewish and secular names are one and the same.

Whatever the case, the key element in terms of Jewish continuity is that the Jewish name given should be the same or very nearly the same as the name of the departed person whom one wants to memorialize in this way.

Misconception: A male baby may be named only at his *Brit* (covenantal circumcision).

The circumcision, which usually takes place on the eighth day, is the standard time when a boy is given his name.

However, there are times when the *Brit* does not take place on the eighth day and in fact may be delayed for quite a while. This is the case when the baby has a severe case of jaundice, is born prematurely, or has an ailment, and the *Brit* must wait until the baby is healthy enough to survive it.

In such instances, it is advisable to give the baby a name at an earlier stage and not wait for the *Brit*. This also gives the added advantage of being able to recite prayers for the baby's recovery, which one would be hard pressed to do were the baby nameless.

In any event, although the *Brit* is the preferable time that the baby be given his name, so his identity and the keeping of the covenant come simultaneously, there are times when this is not possible, and the timing of the event must be adjusted accordingly.

Misconception: Circumcision takes place on the eighth day, because that is the most appropriate time.

Circumcision takes place on the eighth day because that is the time spelled out in the Torah for circumcision.

However, it is questionable whether in fact this is the ideal time for circumcision. If this is the covenantal act of entry into the community of responsibility, it hardly makes sense that one should circumcise the child at the age of eight days. The child has no idea what this is all about, and any covenantal connection is completely lost on the child.

Why then does the circumcision take place on the eighth day? It is the earliest time that the child is healthy enough to tolerate the circumcision, but it is also a time when the child is less likely to feel pain with the intensity he would feel at a later stage. In order to prevent such pain, the circumcision is performed at this early age.

By rights, the circumcision should take place at the time the child has reached the age of responsibility, namely, thirteen. Instead, the child at the age of thirteen, by becoming *bar mitzvah*, reaffirms the covenantal act that was undertaken on his behalf, by his parents, when he was totally unaware.

The *bar mitzvah* is effectively the reaffirmation of the covenant of circumcision, an event the child can hardly be expected to recall.

Misconception: *Mezizah* (sucking out the blood following circumcision) is an archaic practice.

Circumcision involves the cutting off of the foreskin followed by suctioning out the blood in the affected area.

Suctioning may sound like an archaic practice, but this is not the case. Suctioning is designed to remove the blood in as effective a manner as possible and to thereby engender more complete healing at a quicker pace.

Anyone who has a cut a finger and reflexively sucks the wound does so knowing that this is an effective way of stopping the bleeding. The intent of the *mezizah* practice is anything but archaic.

The *mohel* who performs the circumcision thoroughly rinses his mouth with alcohol prior to the suctioning, thereby neutralizing any germ factor. That health precaution ensures that the *mezizah* is carried out without any adverse consequences.

Misconception: There is no reason *mezizah* should be modified.

The original intent of *mezizah* and the precautions taken to ensure its being done properly remain valid. However, the present reality creates serious problems for the continuation of the practice.

That reality includes the explosion of the AIDS (acquired immune deficiency syndrome) epidemic. AIDS is a disease that can be transmitted through the bloodstream. For the purposes of the safety of the *mohel* who does the circumcision, and of the child who is being circumcised, it is wise to avoid doing the *mezizah*, the sucking out of the blood, via direct contact between the circumciser and the child. Instead, it is preferable that this be done through a suction glass, which envelops the area where the circumcision takes place.

Safety and concern for the threat to life are of paramount importance in Judaism. Obliviousness to this in any circumstance, and certainly in the covenant, hardly makes any sense. A covenant is a covenant with life affirmation, not with disease and possible death.

Misconception: In the decision about whether a *Pidyon HaBen* (redemption of the firstborn son) is necessary, the status of the mother's parents is not relevant.

It is a well-known fact of the *Pidyon HaBen* procedure that a child whose father is a *Kohen* or a Levite need not be redeemed. Since the redemption is from the *Kohen*, it hardly makes sense that one who is already part of that larger fraternity would have to engage in the redemption ceremonial.

However, it is not only when the father is a *Kohen* or a Levite that the *Pidyon HaBen* ceremony is rendered superfluous. The same holds true if the child's maternal grandfather is either a *Kohen* or a Levite. In this instance too, the connection with the *Kohen* tribe is so strong as to exempt the family from responsibility to redeem the child.

By the way, the essence of the redemption is a financial responsibility, not the celebration of a partylike occasion. The exemption is therefore not to be seen as a punishment but rather as a great financial relief.

Misconception: It is required that a *Pidyon HaBen* be done with coins.

Ideally, one should redeem one's child with coins. These coins should have a silver weight that adds up to the proper amount contained in the five *shekalim* (plural of *shekel*) that constitute the Torah requirement for redemption of the firstborn.

The amount, which is approximately 100 grams, is not always present in five silver coins. Sometimes one needs to supplement with a sixth coin to be sure that the silver content is adequate.

When one has been unable to secure the right number of silver coins, one may redeem one's firstborn son with a silver tray or other type of silver ornament that contains the 100 grams of silver weight.

The key is that the *Kohen* receive that amount. Since it is an amount based on silver weight, any item that contains this amount of silver, or its equivalent value, suffices.

Misconception: For a *Pidyon HaBen,* it is required that the father be present.

It is highly unlikely that one has ever seen a redemption of the firstborn son without the father's presence.

However, in instances when the father is absent, due either to illness or to being out of town, or the father himself is not in a place where a *Kohen* is available, the father may delegate someone as his agent, to act on his behalf, to redeem his child from the *Kohen* on the appropriate day.

In fact, if the father cannot be back in time and also cannot find a *Kohen* where he is, it is imperative that he appoint someone to act on his behalf, so that the child is redeemed at the appropriate time.

Misconception: For a *Pidyon HaBen*, it is required that the son be present.

It is rare that a *Pidyon HaBen* takes place without the child's presence. However, the essential act of redemption involves giving a certain amount of silver to the *Kohen*, thereby redeeming one's firstborn son. This can be achieved even if the child is not present.

Thus, if a father is far away and cannot get back home in time, it would be more appropriate to find a *Kohen* wherever he is and redeem his son, even though the son who is being redeemed is far away.

In regard to *Pidyon HaBen*, long distance is the next best thing to actually being there.

Misconception: In contemporary times, the firstborn serves no religious function.

In many places in Israel, on a daily basis, and outside Israel, on festivals, the *Kohen*, or group of *Kohanim*, pronounces the blessing as mandated by the Torah.

Prior to their doing this, they are obliged to wash their hands or, more precisely, to have their hands washed. It is the traditional role of the Levites to do this for the *Kohanim*.

However, should there be no Levites present, the firstborn, who originally were destined for service in the sanctuary, assume this role and wash the hands of the *Kohen*.

Being a firstborn does indeed have religious implications.

Misconception: A child who is converted to Judaism is automatically Jewish forever.

Jewish parents who adopt a non-Jewish child will want to make the child an integrally Jewish part of their family and will do so through adoption conversion.

In the case of a male, the dynamics of this process require that the rabbinic court arrange for a circumcision and eventual immersion in the ritual waters known as the *mikvah*. In the case of a female, only the ritual immersion in the *mikvah* water need be arranged. This is all done on the basis of the rabbinic court's charging the parents with the duty of raising the child to fully appreciate Judaic responsibility. This is achieved by the parents themselves, living out that responsibility in their own home.

Technically, it is the obligation of the rabbinic court to raise the child, but that charge is transferred to the parents, who act as the agents of the rabbinic court. This is the essence of the conversion process.

However, this is done without the child's knowledge and agreement. It is hardly fair that parents should thrust upon an innocent child such a great responsibility as being Jewish. Therefore, when the child reaches the age of responsibility, *bar mitzvah* or *bat mitzvah*, the child has the right to renounce the conversion procedure that was entered into on its behalf without its knowledge. Once the child reaches that age and does not renounce the conversion, the conversion becomes valid.

It is wrong to think that the parental adoption procedure is automatically a fact forever. The child does have a voice in what he or she wants to be. The child will want to be Jewish if the parents have transmitted a positive sense of Jewishness.

Misconception: A child who has reached maturity (*bar* or *bat mitzvah*) is culpable for any misdeeds.

Becoming *bar mitzvah* or *bat mitzvah* means becoming responsible to fulfill the commandments. It means that one has the responsibility to actualize and fulfill the precepts. It does not mean that the child therefore is to be condemned for failure to live up to this responsibility. The boy at the age of *bar mitzvah* (entry into fourteenth year) or the girl at the age of *bat mitzvah* (entry into the thirteenth year) is capable of meaningful spiritual activity.

However, the child who does not assume responsibility is not rendered culpable and punishable. For this, a greater level of maturity is necessary; specifically, the child must attain the age of twenty years. It is only then that the child becomes culpable for any misdeeds.

15

Confronting Mortality

Misconception: In Judaic thinking, the human being is
naturally good.

In Judaic thinking, the human being is neither naturally good nor
naturally bad. The human being has propensities for both good and
bad — what are referred to as *yetzer tov* and *yetzer ra*. The human being
is capable of being both good and bad. It is up to him or her to
decide which choice to embrace.

Were the human being naturally bad, it would hardly make
sense to pronounce blame for anything bad that was perpetrated.
Were the human being good, it would hardly make sense to bestow
praise for laudatory behavior. All that human beings achieved
would be an expression of what they are, through no fault or credit
of their own.

The human being who chooses good may then become more
naturally predisposed toward the good. But all the good ensues from
the original choice and is therefore attributable to the human being
and worthy of praise.

The same is true on the other side. A decision toward evil may
very well have long-range consequences, the blame for which is
related to the original opting toward evil and for which the
individual is held responsible.

Misconception: Generally, people die because of a godly decree.

Everyone is destined to die. No one escapes the ultimate decree of life's finality. But the time at which this should occur is certainly in our own hands, to a certain degree. God has the final and ultimate say, but there is reason to believe that what God has to say on this matter is directly related to our own behavior. Consider the talmudic statement that of a hundred people who die, ninety-nine perish as a result of negligence.

If we are urged to be exceedingly heedful of ourselves and to take care of our health, this is a clear statement that how we take care of ourselves will have an effect on our longevity or lack of it.

Every human being works within a destiny, but this does not mean it is an absolute and concrete destiny. It may be a destiny that is related to permutations. Thus, for any specific individual, the destiny chart may read as follows: if the individual smokes three packs of cigarettes a day, the individual will be given fifty years; if two packs of cigarettes a day, fifty-five years; if one pack of cigarettes a day, sixty years; if no cigarettes, seventy-five years.

Cigarette smoking represents a classic case of self-destruction. It makes sense to believe that God's judgment concerning our own lives will take into account how we take care of the life given to us.

If we are true to the trusteeship God has extended to us, God will probably take this into account and reward the individual accordingly. On the other hand, if an individual does not care about life-style, why should God care?

We operate within a specific framework with a broad range. What the options are within that range constitutes the critical factor. The options we choose are in our hands and are significant factors affecting longevity.

Misconception: One may visit the sick at any time during the day.

Visiting the sick is an important act of kindness. However, it must be followed by praying on behalf of the sick person.

If one visits in the first three hours of the day, the sick person may look too good, and the visitor may feel that prayer is not necessary. On the other hand, if the visit is in the last three hours of the day, the sick person may look so awful that the visitor may believe the sick person is beyond hope and may give up.

It is best to visit after the first three hours and before the last three hours of the day, so that the visitor may gain a realistic impression. Translated into modern parlance, the visit should not be too early in the morning or too late at night, but in between.

The visitor is then more likely to pray on behalf of the sick person. Such prayer is a vital component of the *mitzvah* fulfillment in visiting the sick.

Misconception: The most appropriate time to rend a garment for one who has died is just before the funeral.

The appropriate time for rending one's garment for the loss of one of the seven relatives is when one feels the impact of the loss.

Just before the funeral is one such time. It is therefore not inappropriate to rend one's garment then. However, the moment of greatest impact is when one hears the news and learns of the death or is actually present at the passing. That is the first and most appropriate time to rend one's garment and recite the blessing that pronounces God as the True Judge.

Many are either unaware of or unprepared to do this. They rely on the assumption that the later time is available for garment rending and is the more preferred occasion. The first half of that assumption is correct; the second is not.

Misconception: One tears the garment following the death of a parent in the same way one would do for other relatives.

Following the death of a spouse, sibling, or child, the garment is torn on the right side.

Following the death of a parent, the garment is torn on the left side, closer to the heart.

Misconception: Following the death of a parent, one tears only one garment.

The garment that is rent for the parent is torn on the left side, close to the heart.

The heart is crucial for another component of this procedure. The tear must reach to the heart. Thus, for one who is wearing a suit, both the suit jacket and the shirt are torn. However, the undershirt itself is not torn, for reasons related to modesty in appearance, among others.

There are postdeath practices that single out the parents for their special role in making the lives of their children possible.

The tear for a parent reaches to the very core of one's being, to the heart.

Misconception: A tie is the most appropriate garment to rend for a departed relative.

A tie is certainly more appropriate than a ribbon for the rending of a garment following the death of a parent, sibling, spouse, or child.

A ribbon is not a garment at all. It is artificially attached to a garment, and then, in a sort of make-believe, as if the ribbon has just become integrated into the garment, it is torn. After the *shivah* (seven-day period of intense mourning), the ribbon is removed and no mark is left on the shirt or clothing. This makes a mockery of the garment-rending requirement.

Even a tie or scarf is not ideal. The idea of tearing is to project that a part of the person has been torn away. To signify this, a person's basic garment should be torn.

The most basic garment is a shirt or blouse. A tie is not a ribbon, but it is also not as basic as a shirt. One can be dressed without a tie but is quite exposed without a shirt or blouse.

Misconception: If one changes the torn garment in the middle of *shivah,* the fresh garment need not be torn.

There are two components to the regulation concerning the tearing of a garment. One is that the one who is to observe the *shivah* must tear the garment. The second component is that the torn garment must be worn during the entire *shivah* period.

If, for example, the shirt that was torn becomes so dirty that it is not wearable, another used shirt can be worn. However, that shirt must also be torn, so that the mourner still wears a torn garment during the *shivah.*

The tear, as a continuous reminder that an integral part of the mourner has been torn away, must be worn during the entire *shivah* period.

This regulation applies only to the tear for a parent. A change of garment for one of the other relatives does not necessitate a new tear, but such change of garment should nevertheless be avoided.

Misconception: The garment is not torn following death during *Hol HaMoed*.

There are varying customs concerning this. The intermediate days are not ordinary days, but they are also not full festivals. They are in between and lean heavily toward the festival side.

There is no *shivah* (seven days of intense mourning) during this time, and funerals are abbreviated.

In most instances, the tearing of the garment is deferred until the conclusion of the festival. However, following the death of a parent, the garment is torn even on *Hol HaMoed*.

Misconception: When one hears of the passing of a relative for whom one must mourn but whose funeral one cannot attend, one may commence mourning only after the funeral.

Generally, when one hears the news of the passing of a family member, one hardly thinks of immediately beginning the *shivah*. One's thoughts are with the family making preparations and are concerned with staying somewhat in touch with the family during that time.

This is the case even if it is clear that attendance at the funeral will not be possible. Then, having not done anything prior to the funeral, the tendency is to wait for the funeral time and then to be consistent with the family's actual mourning, starting mourning when the rest of the family commences.

However, this is not the only viable alternative. In actuality, once one hears of the passing of a relative whose funeral one will not attend, it is possible to commence *shivah* immediately. After all, the nonattendee is not engaged in any prefuneral preparations, being far away, and probably will not be with the family during the *shivah*.

According to some views, that person may commence the mourning period immediately by tearing the garment upon hearing the news of the death and sitting down and starting the seven days of mourning.

It may seem odd to have the *shivah* commence before the deceased has been buried. But for the one who is at a distance, the farewell takes place as soon as the notification comes and when there is no possibility of attending the final farewell.

Misconception: The garment that is cut for the mourning period must be of a dark color.

The obligation regarding cutting a garment is that one cut a basic article of clothing. In days gone by, some funeral homes glutted the North American public with precut ribbons. This may have saved a garment or two, but it also distorted what the tearing procedure was designed to address.

What would be the proper garment to tear? Ideally, in the mourning situation, the proper garment to tear would be a shirt. The shirt is the most basic garment. It is much more basic than a jacket, which one need not wear all the time, or even a tie, which is simply a decoration upon the shirt. For a woman, the ideal garment to tear would be a blouse or dress.

However, it is well known that very few people who tear shirts go out of their way to buy a black shirt. On the contrary, the shirt that is torn is invariably white. This explodes the myth that one must tear only a dark-colored garment. There are no such color regulations for the shirt or blouse or any other garment that may be torn.

It is inappropriate to dress in loud colors as opposed to subdued colors during the *shivah* period. But it is not necessary to use only dark-colored garments for the tearing procedure.

Misconception: Having a large attendance at the funeral is the main consideration in deciding when the funeral should be held.

Having a large attendance at the funeral is not an insignificant matter. Scheduling the funeral for a time when very few people can attend is unfair to the deceased.

Sparse attendance may be interpreted as a sad commentary on the life of the deceased and is a painful sight for the family, just as a large attendance may be a pleasant commentary on the deceased's life and a source of comfort to the family.

But the expected size of the crowd attending the funeral is not the major consideration in deciding when the funeral should be held. The dignity of the deceased as spelled out in Jewish law is the prime arbiter. One element of that dignity is to have the funeral and burial as soon as possible.

If death occurred on Thursday evening, for example, the family may prefer to defer the funeral until Sunday, when more people may attend. But that would extend the interval between death and burial to three days. This is considered an indignity to the deceased, whose burial should not be delayed for such a long time.

Misconception: A *Kohen* may always attend the funeral of a sister.

A sister is one of the seven basic relatives. These seven relatives are the persons whom one formally mourns after their passing, through observing the *shivah* and the post-*shivah* protocol.

These seven relatives are also the ones whose funeral a *Kohen* may attend. However, if the sister was married, then the *Kohen* may no longer be in the proximity of his sister, should she die. This is the exception to the rule.

The *Kohen* maintains the mourning period even for his married sister but does not take part in the funeral.

It should be noted with caution that "attending the funeral" refers to being in the same room with the deceased, or within four cubits (about six feet) of the deceased, and walking into the cemetery. It is possible, via microphone hookup, for the *Kohen* to hear all that transpires during the funeral, without actually being in the funeral chapel.

Misconception: What today is called a eulogy was in previous generations called a *hesped*.

The relationship between a eulogy and a *hesped* is parallel to the relationship between a sigh and a cry.

The traditional *hesped* was an occasion, usually a funeral, when all those in attendance were in tears. Professional criers would wail away and create a mood of such profound sadness that only the most insensitive remained dry eyed.

The words of the *maspid* (the one making the *hesped*) added spiritual fuel to the emotional fire.

By comparison, the modern eulogy is more a biographical recitation and listing of credits. It is not without merit, but it is not a *hesped*.

This fact is important not only for its own sake. It is vital to the issue of what to do when a *hesped* is forbidden, such as on *Rosh Hodesh* or *Hol HaMoed*.

A bland eulogy on those days is not prohibited as is the more mournful *hesped*.

Misconception: A lengthy discourse of intricate Torah scholarship is an appropriate way to eulogize a deceased person.

The most appropriate way to eulogize a deceased person is to speak pointedly, directly, and effectively about the deceased. The eulogy should speak of the achievements of the deceased and the values he or she espoused.

Pilpulistic discourses that digress far afield and only eventually return to the subject at hand are less than ideal. Such presentations often lack proper focus, and they lose the audience in a maze of intellectual intrigue.

Such presentations may also be contrary to *halakhah*, which forbids the study of Torah in the presence of a deceased individual. Such study mocks the poor—the poor being the deceased, who cannot engage in Torah study.

Misconception: Covering the casket with earth after interment is cruel and insensitive.

There are some who argue that the quicker one completes the funeral service, the better. At burial, the argument goes, it would be more appropriate to lower the casket, cover it, recite the *Kaddish*, and return home. As much as this argument may be rooted in sensitive concern for the bereaved family, it is nevertheless ill informed.

The culminating respect that must be accorded to the deceased includes proper and complete burial. Relatives and friends take shovel in hand to lovingly cover the deceased's resting place. This is painful, but it is vital and proper.

Most people would shudder in horror if they were to witness what actually happens when the grave is not covered. Usually, a bulldozer is brought to dump the earth into the grave. That is insensitive, even insulting. Seeing this once is enough to convince the doubters about the wisdom of the Judaic interment protocol.

But there is more to this than avoiding the bulldozer. However painful may be the personal involvement in and actual witnessing of the burial, the fact that it is the halakhic, and therefore respectful, way is an ultimate comfort to the family.

Also, the pain involved in personally witnessing the burial helps the surviving family to directly confront their loss — in psychological parlance, to do their grief work. Avoiding this confrontation is harmful in the long run, as it may result in the serious depression that sometimes ensues from unresolved grief.

16

Mourning

Misconception: The condolence meal must be provided for the mourners by others as an act of communal kindness.

The mourners, when returning from the funeral, are provided with sustenance by family and friends. They are forbidden to eat the first meal from their own food. They must be taken care of by the community.

This is obviously an act of communal kindness, but its purpose is more related to the situation of the mourners. The mourners are focused on the mourning and probably give very little thought to eating. The community must relieve them of this responsibility so that they can direct their attention to the mourning.

Alternatively, because of the trauma that the mourners are enduring, there is a strong likelihood that they will have no appetite. By making the community provide them with food, we are more assured that they will eat.

There is a kindness component to what the community does, but the essential thrust of this communal responsibility is more focused on the mourners than it is on the general community.

Misconception: For the *Seudat Havraah* (condolence meal) following a funeral, the main ingredient is the egg.

The condolence meal following the funeral is a meal given by family and friends to the mourners. The egg, as a round object, symbolizes the cycle of life, that life is a circle, and that the mourner, who is now on a downside of the cycle, will, it is hoped, be comforted and eventually latch onto the upper part of the cycle. As such, the egg, or any other round food, indeed has a powerful symbolic meaning for the bereaved. However, the main ingredient of the condolence meal is not the egg or any other round food. The main ingredient is bread. The communal charge to provide the condolence meal is not fulfilled if bread is not part of the meal.

Misconception: Mourners observe the *shivah* to honor the deceased.

The intent of the *shivah* period is for the survivors to fully absorb their loss and to gradually come out of the shock, the trauma, and the despair, to appreciate human life.

It is an honor to the memory of the deceased when the survivors study, give charity, or perform other good deeds in his or her memory.

The *shivah* may conduce to this, but it is more a by-product of the sitting than a reflection of the main intent.

Misconception: When the *shivah* is observed, all mourners will always observe the same seven days of mourning.

Under normal circumstances, the mourners will get together and their period of mourning will be the same. But this is not always the case.

Consider the situation when the deceased is transported to interment far away from the place of the funeral. For example, the body of someone who passes away in North America and who is eulogized there may then be taken to Israel for burial.

Some members of the family may accompany the deceased while others remain behind. Those who remain must start their *shivah* immediately upon departing from the deceased. Those who go to Israel will begin their mourning only from the time of the burial.

Those who have been notified of a death but who cannot attend the funeral may assume the *shivah* immediately, even if the funeral has not yet taken place. Those who attend the funeral begin the *shivah* after the funeral.

These are a number of examples of situations in which various members of the family observe different seven-day periods of mourning.

Misconception: A mourner who joins a *shivah* in progress will continue *shivah* after the others have concluded.

If the *shivah* in progress includes the head of the household — the one who is the acknowledged leader of the surviving family and the one upon whom rests the responsibility for the burial and other family matters — the family member joining the *shivah* will slide into the in-progress *shivah*, concluding the *shivah* with the family.

This is the case if the mourner joined the *shivah* in the middle or even toward the end.

If that same mourner decides to observe the *shivah* alone, commencing the *shivah* later than the rest of the family, that mourner must observe the *shivah* for the full seven days.

Misconception: In choosing a place to sit during *shivah*, a higher chair is preferable to a lower couch.

The human being normally sits on a chair, consistent with the usually majestic feeling linked to being part of God's world.

A mourner, on the other hand, feels anything but majestic. A mourner feels devastated and low, and mourning practices at once create a mood and reinforce a mood.

The prescription regarding sitting during the mourning period is a case in point. The mourner must move off the lofty perch and onto a low seat, consistent with the low feeling that pervades the mourner. Some actually sit on the floor.

The key is to sit low and, after the *shivah,* to rise from that low.

There is no law that one must be uncomfortable during mourning, merely low. Thus, a lower couch is preferable to a higher chair, especially if it is an ordinary chair, which is usually higher than the twelve-inch maximum for mourning chairs.

Misconception: During *shivah*, mourners may eat meals on regular chairs at a regular table.

Many people find it uncomfortable to eat on a low stool at a regular table. They therefore assume it is permissible to eat their meals during the *shivah* period at a regular table, on regular chairs.

This is a wrong conclusion. The mourner must eat, but even during meals must not lose sight of the fact that this is a mourning period.

In addition, when mourners eat at the regular table, usually with other family members and friends, the atmosphere of mourning becomes compromised. It feels almost like a family gathering.

Jewish tradition has no problem with family gatherings, but at the right time. During *shivah*, mourners should sit in a mourning position when eating.

Misconception: *Nihum avelim* (comforting of mourners) is directly linked to the *shivah*.

Under normal circumstances, the time for comforting the mourners is during the seven-day mourning period.

Specifically, the time for beginning to visit mourners, to alleviate their intense grief, is from the morning of the third day following the funeral.

For example, if the funeral is on Monday, and the *shivah* starts on Monday afternoon, then by Wednesday morning, *shivah* visitation is in order.

This is in the normal mode of things. However, there are occasions, rare but nevertheless real, when comforting of mourners is possible even though *shivah* has not begun.

The specific instance when this arises is when a death occurs prior to the festival or during the festival — and the burial takes place in the intermediate days — of either Sukkot or Pesah.

In these circumstances, the start of *shivah* is delayed until after the conclusion of the festival. However, even though the family is technically not in a *shivah* state following the burial, they are nevertheless obviously traumatized by what has happened. It is therefore fitting and proper for friends and relatives to visit with the family and to comfort them, even though the family is not yet in the midst of the *shivah* period.

This is a fulfillment of the *mitzvah* to comfort mourners. Comforting mourners is an obligation that is therefore independent of the *shivah*.

Misconception: *Shivah* can never be completed before burial.

Usually, *shivah* starts only after burial. Even when burial takes place in another city, the time interval between the funeral and burial is only a few days at most.

However, there is a unique circumstance when *shivah* precedes burial. This is when a person is lost through a terrorist act, a kidnapping, or a suspected but not proven fatal accident.

At the point in time when the family has given up hope that the lost person is alive, they begin the *shivah* period.

Should the body be found later on, whether it be weeks, months, or years, it is buried with full dignity. However, since the family has already observed *shivah*, it need not do so again.

In this instance, the *shivah* precedes burial. This is obviously not a likely occurrence, but it is also not impossible.

338

Misconception: Saying to someone in mourning, "You should have no more sorrow," is an appropriate wish.

There is no doubt that those who wish mourners they "should have no more sorrow" do so with a full and sincere heart. They are overwhelmed by the devastation that is felt by the mourners and are moved to express a wish that the mourners will no longer have to encounter such pain.

The wish contained in the expression, as sincere and genuine as it may be, is nevertheless wanting. How is it possible for an individual to live and have no sorrow? Sorrow is part of life.

To wish that someone will have no more sorrow is to unwittingly wish for that individual not to live much longer, so as to avoid the encounter with any more sorrow. This is the case because unfortunately the only way one can avoid sorrow is by avoiding life. And the only way one can avoid life is by dying.

It turns out that the wish to have no more sorrow is authentic, genuine, and sincere, but wrong.

It would be more appropriate to express the hope that the mourners will have many pleasant occasions in their future, or some other well-intentioned and well-reasoned hope.

Misconception: It is acceptable to greet others — nonmourners — in the house of mourning.

The house of mourning is not a place for socialization. It is a house of sorrow, a house of confrontation with that sorrow, a house that is serious in its focus on coming to grips with what has occurred.

Normal conversational flow is not appropriate in a house of mourning. It is not business as usual, with hellos and good-byes to the mourner, as if the dialogue with the mourner is ordinary conversation.

In addition, those who are visiting the mourners, who greet others in the house of mourning with ordinary hellos and how-are-yous, show an insensitivity to those in mourning. They must appreciate that the house of mourning is not a place for the regular communication pattern.

The house of mourning is different not only for the mourners but also for everyone else.

Misconception: A mourner should not take a nap during the *shivah*.

The *shivah* period carries with it many precise regulations concerning what may and may not be done during this time.

The general rule is that one must focus on the loss and on how to integrate the memory of the deceased into one's life. Any activity that deflects from this is off limits during this time. Thus, one may not engage in business or become involved in intense study, even of Torah.

However, this does not mean that one may not eat or that one must remain awake for all this time. The logic that during sleep one cannot focus on the mourning is not a serious argument. After all, even during *shivah*, one needs to live and to take care of fundamental needs.

This also applies to the need to relax by taking a nap. If one is physically tired or mentally exhausted, there is no reason to force oneself to stay awake. A nap during the day for these reasons is as legitimate as sleep at night.

Misconception: Only mourners must sit on low seats during *shivah*.

It is common practice that those visiting mourners to comfort them sit on ordinary chairs. They do so as a matter of course, without hesitation.

But by rights, those visiting should also sit on low stools, to empathically assume the same position as the mourners.

Over time, this primary and wise rule has fallen by the wayside, mainly because the mourners themselves are not insistent on the protocol and allow visitors to sit as they please.

However the practice has evolved, it is still vital to remember the basic law and the implications of that law. One may sit higher than the mourner but should empathize on the mourner's level.

Misconception: It is proper to bring food to mourners during *shivah*.

It has become common practice among many to bring food to the mourners during *shivah*. For some who do not know what to do for the mourners, this is a vital option.

However, this practice is at the very least questionable. Consider the ruling that one is enjoined from sending *manot* on Purim to a mourner in the thirty days following the death of a relative other than a parent. To one who is mourning a parent, one should not send these *manot* for the full twelve months. This latter restriction is subject to some leniency in places where ordinary greetings are extended during the twelve-month mourning period.

It is clear that sending a gift of food to a mourner is prohibited even after the more intense first seven days. In effect, this renders the custom of sending food during *shivah* problematic.

However, should such food be sent, the mourner need not reject the gift, obviously sent with good intentions.

It should also be clear that all this is relevant only when the mourners have enough food. For poor mourners, for whom the food package fills an immediate need, giving food falls into the category of charity to ward off possible starvation.

In most cases, when food is sent, the mourners have so much that a good portion of it goes to waste. This is another variable that well-intentioned friends and family should contemplate before sending food.

Also, it is important that whoever sends or brings the food, in instances when this is proper, should merely put it down on a table rather than giving it directly to any of the mourners.

Misconception: A mourner may not finalize an engagement in the middle of *shivah*.

Matchmaking—putting people together to fuse the building blocks of Jewish continuity—is a holy endeavor. It is an endeavor that knows of little restriction.

Because it is so important, and because an opportunity missed may never be recaptured, one is permitted to finalize an engagement even in the *shivah* period.

The celebration of such a match must obviously be deferred, but making the match is not deferred, and if necessary, can even be concretized on the day of death.

Misconception: Regarding mourning regulations, rabbis and cantors are the same as everyone else.

___

One of the features of the mourning period is that the mourners do not sit in their regular seats in the *Bet Knesset* for the duration of the mourning period.

At the same time, one is not permitted to exhibit public mourning on the *Shabbat*.

One who moves up or down one row in the *Bet Knesset* will probably do so without drawing much attention.

However, if a rabbi or cantor in mourning moved to a different seat, this would be noticed. Such a move on the *Shabbat* would contravene the regulation that no public mourning is to be exhibited on *Shabbat*.

A rabbi or cantor in mourning should remain in the regular *Shabbat* seat. Thus, rabbis and cantors who are in mourning are not the same as everyone else.

Misconception: Mourners may not attend public prayer services on Tishah B'Av.

Under normal circumstances, mourners are not permitted to leave the house of mourning during the seven-day mourning period, with the obvious exception of *Shabbat*, when no public manifestation of mourning is exhibited.

A mourner who cannot gather a *minyan* at home may likewise go directly to the *Bet Knesset* to pray and then immediately return home to resume the *shivah*.

There is another notable exception to the rule that mourners must remain in the house of mourning. That exception is Tishah B'Av. On that day, the entire community of Israel is in mourning. Even though they are in mourning, they obviously still attend services in the *Bet Knesset*.

The mourner for a loved one whose mourning period coincides with Tishah B'Av is no different from anyone else and may attend services in the *Bet Knesset*.

Misconception: A person in the midst of *shivah* may not be called to the Torah on Tishah B'Av.

Tishah B'Av is a day of intense national mourning. The entire community of Israel laments the destruction of the *Bet HaMikdash*, which occurred twice around Tishah B'Av.

The community mourns the destruction, the resultant thrust into exile, and the subsequent calamities that unfolded through that exile.

On Tishah B'Av, everyone is a mourner. Everyone is literally observing a *shivah*-type mourning for our people.

The individual who is in the midst of a personal *shivah* is thus no different from other community members. All are in intense mourning. All are equal regarding being called to the Torah. All may be called.

17

Mourning after Mourning

Misconception: There is no restriction on greeting a mourner after the *shivah*.

Even though the mourner who concludes the *shivah* period of intense mourning returns to a regular routine, this does not mean everything returns to normal.

The wounds are still open, and the healing process has just barely begun. Greeting a mourner just after *shivah* with a cheery hello, as if nothing has transpired, is at the very least callous.

Any greeting in the post-*shivah* time frame, at least till the conclusion of the thirty-day period of less intense mourning called *sheloshim*, must take into account the mourner's state of mind.

Such greeting should therefore be understated, sensitive, and suffused with empathy.

Misconception: One who has been interred in the wrong grave should not be moved to an appropriate burial place.

To be buried in the wrong place is considered an indignity to the deceased that must be corrected.

This is obviously the case if the grave belongs to someone else, or if the deceased is buried without permission in a field, and the property owner refuses to sell the burial spot to the family of the person interred.

It is also the case even in a circumstance when the burial took place with the permission of the property owner, but said owner refuses to sell the burial site property. The deceased is in property belonging to someone else and was not interred without permission. It is just that ownership of the burial site has not been given over to the deceased.

The notion that a person should be interred in a place that belongs to the deceased is important enough that moving to such a locale is permissible.

In instances when a person is mistakenly buried in another's plot, no effort should be spared to correct the situation through some arrangement with the owner of the plot. If all effort fails, then the wrongly interred must be moved, since no one has the right to take someone else's plot.

To be interred in a plot that belongs to another is a lingering blight on the deceased, a blight that must be corrected.

Misconception: There is no mandated mourning when reinterring a body.

The day a body is taken for reburial is quite traumatic. It is natural that this represents an emotional time for the family and is certainly not an ordinary day.

The feeling is reinforced by the regulation that the day of reinterment, from the moment the first grave is opened until evening, be considered a day of mandated mourning, with the intensity of *shivah*, for the immediate family.

The mourners also rend the garment (*kriyah*) on the day of reinterment.

The mourning lasts only for the day of reinterment.

Misconception: It is better that the son recite the *Kaddish* (sanctification affirmation after death) even though he makes many mistakes in the recitation.

The *Kaddish* is a glorification and sanctification of God. It is the statement of hope that is recited precisely at the time when one feels forlorn and needs a reinforcement of hope.

As well intentioned as this recitation may be, if it is fraught with error, it is something less than a sanctifying and glorifying prayer. It borders on being a disgrace to God.

Today, with the availability of many useful educational tools, it does not take too long to master the proper recitation of the *Kaddish*. Even one who does not know Hebrew can easily master the transliteration of the *Kaddish* and appreciate its meaning.

There is therefore no excuse for engaging in the jawbreaking exercise of reciting a *Kaddish* that, intended as a sanctification, becomes anything but a sanctification.

The son should learn to say the *Kaddish* properly before reciting it in public.

Misconception: Women may not recite *Kaddish*.

Women are not required to recite the *Kaddish* said during prayer services following the death of a parent, spouse, sibling, or child, much the same way as they are not required to attend prayer services.

However, they may recite the *Kaddish* if they so desire and should certainly not be disparaged for this.

It is also highly advisable for women in mourning who do not recite the *Kaddish* to carefully listen to the *Kaddish* as it is being evoked in the congregational setting and to make the proper responses in the course of the *Kaddish* recitation. This is considered equivalent to actually having said the *Kaddish*.

Misconception: Music is the main impediment to attending a wedding when in mourning.

Most people assume that the major problem with attending a wedding during the mourning period is that there is music. They devise elaborate schemes for getting around this problem, such as eating and then leaving as soon as the music starts.

All this is based on a mistake. The main impediment to attending a wedding is the wedding itself. The joy of the occasion and the camaraderie of a joyous nature run contrary to the theme of the mourning period, which must be sober, serious, and focused on the deceased.

There are, of course, certain circumstances wherein one may attend a wedding even when in mourning. But it should be understood that the major problem to be addressed is not the music but the actual event.

Other joyous events, such as birthday parties and anniversaries, which may have no music, still are off limits during the mourning period, specifically because they are occasions of rejoicing, when the mourner should be in a more contemplative mode.

Misconception: There is nothing wrong with leaning on a monument in a cemetery.

The monument is set up for a dedicated purpose: to serve as the indicator of who resides in the burial place. Family and friends thus have a clear and respectful signpost as a directional compass for them as they go to pray at the grave site.

One may not derive any benefit from such a monument. Leaning on it is clearly a benefit and is therefore forbidden.

Misconception: One cannot have a *Hakamat Matzayvah* (establishing a monument for the deceased) without a rabbi.

The major ingredients of a *Hakamat Matzayvah* are (1) recitation of appropriate prayers, (2) delivery of a fitting tribute about the deceased, (3) recitation of the memorial prayer, and (4) recitation of the sanctification prayer called *Kaddish*.

A rabbi on site will more likely ensure that these ingredients are manifest at the *Hakamat Matzayvah* and that they are properly expressed. But all this can be done without a rabbi. A family member or close personal friend may express a fitting tribute, the entire assemblage may recite psalms, and the memorial prayer can be said rather than sung.

A rabbi helps, as does a cantor. But their presence is not required.

Misconception: There is no real significance to placing stones on a cemetery monument.

Placing stones at the grave site is a time-honored tradition. It signifies that a visitor has been to the grave site. On the basis of one stone per visitor, many stones constitute a sign of appreciation for the life of the deceased.

This is of significant solace to the family and a fitting tribute of manifest proportions to the deceased.

Misconception: One properly observes a *Yahrzeit* (yearly anniversary of the death) merely by reciting *Kaddish* and lighting a candle.

Lighting a candle is a vital part of the observance of the *Yahrzeit*, the date that a loved one passed away and that is commemorated each year. The flickering flame is reminiscent of the soul and is a potent reminder of the tenuousness of life. Also, the flame gives off light, even as the deceased still illumines with the legacy that lives.

The *Kaddish* too is important, as it affirms unwavering commitment to God and the godly values ennobled in life by the deceased and hopefully enlarged upon by his or her posterity.

But the perfunctory kindling of a light and recitation of *Kaddish* do not capture the essence of *Yahrzeit*. *Yahrzeit* gains its full meaning through understanding why these observances are so basic. This makes the *Yahrzeit* day one of profound, meaningful significance.

It is customary to fast on the *Yahrzeit*, to thereby transform this day into a time for soul-searching and self-improvement. In addition, *Yahrzeit* is a day to visit the grave, engage in Torah study, and do charitable deeds in memory of the departed, thereby honoring the deceased's memory.

There is more to *Yahrzeit* than meets the eye. *Yahrzeit* must meet the soul.

Misconception: There are no food restrictions on the day of *Yahrzeit*.

The day of *Yahrzeit*, especially that of one's parents, is no ordinary day. Even years after their deaths, one is obliged to actively commemorate the parents' memory on the day of their passing (the *Yahrzeit* day).

On that day, one should avoid parties and other displays of levity. In fact, it is customary to fast on the *Yahrzeit* day. Those who for whatever reason cannot fast should at the very least abstain from meat and wine.

Whatever the extent, it is clear that *Yahrzeit* carries with it specific protocols that should be honored.

Misconception: One who forgets to observe the *Yahrzeit* must wait until the following year before doing so.

It sometimes happens that an individual realizes toward the end of the day of the *Yahrzeit* that the *Yahrzeit* commemoration has been forgotten. The immediate question is, What should one do?

Obviously, one cannot go back in time. But it is also not the case that one has to wait until the following year to observe the *Yahrzeit*.

Even though observing it the next day is not the same as observing the *Yahrzeit* on the actual day, it is appropriate for the individual to observe the *Yahrzeit* on the day immediately after one has remembered that the *Yahrzeit* was forgotten.

Misconception: If a number of people are observing *Yahrzeit*, it is correct to give preference to a sage for being called to the Torah.

Under normal circumstances, the sage in the community is the most highly respected, the one to whom one must show greatest deference. Logic would therefore militate for calling the sage to the Torah for *Yahrzeit*, ahead of others not as sage who are also observing *Yahrzeit*.

However, this is not the case. On the contrary, concerning the *Aliyah*, preference should be given to those who are not sage. This not only seems illogical but also is to a certain extent contrary to common practice.

However, what at first glance seems to be illogical has an eminent logic to it. First, the sage has many ways by which to commemorate the *Yahrzeit*, most notably through the study of Torah, which the sage has already presumably done in abundance. On the other hand, the nonsage may not have such an option and may not even think of it. For that person, the only avenue for true commemoration, aside from recitation of the *Kaddish*, may be through being called to the Torah for an *Aliyah*.

Second, the sage will understand that not having an *Aliyah* is not that disastrous, precisely because there are other alternatives, whereas the less-schooled individual may see the lack of an *Aliyah* as insulting, even devastating.

For these logical and well-balanced reasons, it is preferable to give the *Aliyah* to the nonsage.

18

Business Ethics

Misconception: Jewish courts for litigation are not operative outside Israel.

In most cities with large Jewish populations, there are Jewish courts ready to adjudicate monetary disputes between individuals. It is appropriate to go to these courts for such litigation and for the parties involved to submit in advance to the judgment of the rabbinical tribunal and abide by their ruling. They should not contest the ruling in a civil court if the decision of the rabbinical tribunal is not to their liking.

This also has the advantage of taking a severe load off the already overburdened civil court system.

Misconception: There is no problem associated with settling monetary disputes in a civil court.

The rules of law in a civil court do not always correlate with the law in a Jewish court. Even elementary items such as excess profits are clear instances wherein Jewish law differs from civil law. There are also differences in many other matters.

Submitting a case to a civil court opens up the likelihood that the adjudication will be inconsistent with Jewish law. If that unfolds, it could be tantamount to stealing or taking from someone else what Jewish law would not have awarded.

Even were that not at issue, the forsaking of the Torah and the search elsewhere for adjudication is considered a most serious offense.

Misconception: The actions of a drunken person are not legally binding.

The transactions, meaning buying or selling, of a person who is drunk are legally binding.

However, should one reach the state of "Lot's drunkenness," with no awareness whatsoever of what one is doing, such a drunken one is in the category of the insane, whose actions are not legally binding.

This does not mean that a drunken person is not responsible for damage inflicted while intoxicated. The person should be aware that there will be no relaxation of culpability for having inflicted damage when drunk.

The idea that being intoxicated is no excuse may serve to sober up some budding alcoholics.

Misconception: A person is always liable for damage inflicted when asleep.

A person who falls asleep and during sleep inflicts damage is obligated to make recompense for the damage.

Unlike the drunkard, who is guilty of having become drunk in the first place, the person who has fallen asleep has really committed no crime. However, the basic Judaic principle that a person is always responsible for actions applies to both the waking state and the sleeping state.

A person who inflicts damage in a sleeping state is obligated to make recompense, even though the person is not guilty of any crime or misdemeanor in falling asleep.

However, there are instances when an individual who has fallen asleep would be exonerated from paying for damage. For example, if after having fallen asleep, someone else moved into the vicinity of the person who was asleep and suffered some damage, the sleeper could not be held responsible. This is because when the sleeper fell asleep, there was no one nearby, and the sleeper had no way of knowing that someone would come and place himself or herself within reach of the sleeper.

Misconception: One who inflicts damage on another person need make only financial recompense.

Monetary recompense to a victim is the primary amends a victimizer must make to compensate for the wrongful action. However, that in itself is not sufficient. The inflictor of damage must also seek out the victim and ask the victim's forgiveness.

Financial amends take care of the monetary loss but do not address the emotional pain and anguish caused to the victim. For that, the personal approach to ask for forgiveness from the victim is necessary and legally required.

Misconception: There is no problem related to paying in advance for the purchase of an item.

Payment in advance is not without some serious potential problems. There is the possibility that by the time the item is delivered, the price of the item will have gone up. To then accept the item at the lower price would seem to be an interest payment for having paid in advance.

This seems contradictory to the norms of commerce, but it projects an indication of how careful and painstaking Jewish law is with regard to taking interest.

If the seller has immediately in hand the items that were sold, the advance payment poses no problem, since it is as if the goods had been immediately transferred.

Another instance that does not pose a problem occurs when there is a fixed market price for the goods at the time of purchase. Since the buyer could have purchased this item almost anywhere, it is considered as if the buyer has the items in hand, and the interest problem is avoided.

Failing these contingencies, there is a serious problem associated with paying in advance.

Misconception: One may sell inferior goods as superior quality if one reduces the price.

When one sells inferior goods as being of superior quality, that is fraud. Even the fact that one sells the goods at a reduced price does not detract from the fraud.

It may be true that had the buyer known the goods were second class, he or she would have paid the reduced price for them.

All this misses the point. The point is that saying something is what it is not constitutes deceit and fraud and is forbidden.

Misconception: If one offers to buy an item for more than it is worth, the vendor need not advise the prospective buyer of its true value.

Since it is the buyer who is offering to purchase the item for more than it is worth, it would seem as if the seller cannot be accused of deceit, since it was not the seller who established the price; it was the buyer.

Nevertheless, it is the obligation of the vendor to tell the buyer what is the current price. If after having been so advised the buyer still insists on paying the higher price, then that is acceptable. But the seller who knows what is the actual price must relate that information to the buyer.

Misconception: Bargaining down a seller with unfounded claims that the item may be bought cheaper elsewhere is acceptable practice.

There is a prohibition against overcharging. There is also a prohibition against underpaying. Deliberately misleading a vendor by saying that the item for sale is available for a cheaper price elsewhere, when this is not the case, will probably cause the vendor to lower the price. But this is an artificial lowering that has been caused by a lie. The buyer is guilty of using devious practices, underpaying, and unfairly denying to the vendor what is due.

What may be common business practice is not acceptable Jewish business ethics.

Misconception: If a vendor, out of ignorance, offers a valuable item at a low price, the knowledgeable prospective buyer need not say anything.

This proposition is the classic definition of bargain hunting. One is always excited about "getting a steal."

But if when purchasing an item for an obviously low price the buyer knows the vendor is not aware of its true value, as may occur with the sale of, say, an antique, a classic edition of a book, or a painting, that buyer must indicate to the prospective seller what the market rate is for the item.

This would likewise apply to any current rage, say, sports trading cards, which have a wide range of prices.

It is nice to get a bargain, but not by obviously and deliberately fooling someone. Such acquisition of a bargain may provide a temporary thrill, but it is fraught with long-range negative implications.

Misconception: One who has agreed to work for an employer may not back out of that agreement.

An employer may not back out of a work agreement with a prospective employee. However, this does not apply in the reverse. An employee who has a agreement to work for an employer may back out of that agreement on the proviso that this does not cause the employer damage.

The basic reasoning for this is that all individuals retain their freedom and cannot be forced into a servitude against their will.

This is not to say that this is recommended practice — only that an employee who backs out of an agreement with an employer and does not cause the employer any damage has the right to do so.

Misconception: An employee need not consider health habits relevant to the job at hand.

Obviously the obligation to maintain one's health is a primary directive of Jewish life. But even independent of this general directive, there is a special ethical responsibility related to the robust health one should be in on the job.

If an individual is not fully able to do the job at hand, that individual is shortchanging the employer. If to do an honest day's work, one needs sufficient rest the day prior, the ethical guidelines of employment dictate that the employee gain sufficient rest in order to honestly carry out the agreed-upon tasks.

Misconception: There are no significant problems connected to the borrowing of articles.

Consider the situation of someone who needed a case of tuna fish or salmon when the stores were closed. The person then borrowed it from a neighbor.

If at the time of this favor a case of salmon or tuna was worth fifty dollars, but by the time the case is returned the price of a new case has gone up to fifty-five or sixty dollars, this turns into a situation of repaying with interest, because the item returned is now worth more than the item that was lent out in the first place.

This does not mean one must cease and desist from lending articles to others. However, care should be given to the possibility that the prohibition against interest may arise. If the price is the same upon return of the cans of tuna, obviously there is no problem.

The best way to avoid any potential difficulty is to state at the moment of transfer that the debt is for the return of the value of the goods rather than the exact number of the goods. This way, interest problems will be avoided.

The problem of disparity would also arise if the original item had been purchased at a deep discount, and the item to be returned, whether a radio, a chair, or a book, were bought at a normal price. This too smacks of interest and poses great problems.

Misconception: It is permissible to levy a penalty for the late payment of a loan.

Many banks and charge card companies do levy such penalties. However, for individuals to do so to others whom they have granted a loan would be considered interest on the loan and is therefore absolutely forbidden.

If only credit card companies and banks followed this rule.

Misconception: An item of security for a loan can be used to repay the loan, no matter what its value.

If the security used to repay a loan is worth more than the value of the loan, by paying back the loan with that security, one is effectively paying the lender more than was borrowed. This is, by definition, interest.

It does not make a difference whether the direct payment of interest is in actual money or its equivalent. As long as the repayment is for more than the actual loan, it is interest and therefore forbidden.

An item of security can be used to repay the loan only if it is not worth more than the actual value of the loan itself, or if the lender returns to the borrower the difference in value between the security and the loan.

Misconception: There is no problem in repaying a loan with goods that are assessed at a reduced value.

Goods that are assessed at a reduced value and then used to repay a loan open up the concern about paying back a loan with interest.

Suppose the loan is for one thousand dollars. Suppose the borrower would like to pay back with goods, for example, a computer that is really worth fourteen hundred dollars but that, for the purposes of repayment, is assessed as being worth exactly one thousand dollars.

If this is a fictional assessment for repayment purposes, but the item, here the computer, is actually worth more, then by repaying with the computer, one is repaying with interest. This should be avoided.

Misconception: As a means of protection from inflation, one may arrange the repayment of a loan through index-linked payments.

Many people today are sensitive to the bite inflation takes out of the dollar. To protect against this, in the case of a loan, they build in the protection of indexing.

Thus, if the inflation rate is 10 percent, the value of a thousand dollars is down to around nine hundred in terms of buying power. By indexing the payments, the borrower will pay back more in pure dollars, even though it may amount to the same in buying power.

However, since the payment is for more than the original loan, the excuse that the buying power reduction necessitates this over-payment is rejected. This is considered interest on a loan and therefore is prohibited.

Misconception: There can be no objection to a loan society's restricting its services to dues-paying members only.

Loan societies have long been a part of the social network that is geared to help those in need. Loan societies that allow only their members to secure loans are perfectly legitimate, as long as membership in the society is free. However, if membership in the society can be gained only through paying dues, this effectively means that one can secure a loan only through having made a payment for that privilege.

This payment is tantamount to paying interest for a loan. Especially is this the case for someone who comes to the society asking for a loan and is told by the director that the only way the loan can be secured is if the would-be borrower pays the membership fee in advance.

It makes no difference what the payment is called. It may be called a membership fee or it may be called a service charge. It all amounts to the same thing, namely, paying more than the actual amount of the loan for the loan.

No matter what it is labeled, it is interest and therefore is forbidden.

Misconception: There is no problem associated with returning the favor of having been invited to a meal.

This is common practice. People feel indebted to those who have invited them to a meal and therefore feel obligated to return the favor. However, returning such a favor smacks of repaying a debt — not a legal debt but more of a moral debt.

Should the individual who returns the invitation do so with a more sumptuous meal, this may be construed as interest payment on a debt, raising the issue of the prohibition against any interest. This may seem a bit extreme, but it shows the extent to which Jewish law abhors the taking of interest in any way, shape, or form.

Explicitly asking someone to "eat with me what you had previously fed to me" gives the appearance of repaying a debt. If more is served at the return meal than at the original meal, it smacks of interest.

Such invitational language should not be used.

Misconception: Mail-order gift incentives are acceptable practice.

A Jewish mail-order firm that offers a gift as incentive for buying in advance — and the customer can either keep or return the items purchased — engages in a highly questionable practice.

If the goods are returned and the money refunded, in retrospect the money sent by the buyer is seen as a loan. The gift is then interest for "granting the loan."

If the goods are kept, the gift becomes interest for paying in advance.

Either way, this practice is too interest laden to be acceptable.

Misconception: In the promotional advertising for a product, it is permissible to knock the competition.

Although it is common practice to knock the competition as a way of increasing sales, Jewish law does not allow this. It is one thing to point out the superiority of the product one has for sale, the service that comes with it, or the better price. It is another to point out that the competition is selling an inferior product or selling it at unfair prices.

This is in the category of evil talk of others, which is prohibited and may not be employed as a business practice.

Misconception: There is nothing wrong with offering to buy from another's belongings what one desires to possess.

Often, on venturing into another person's house, one sees an item one likes. When it is a rare item that is no longer available, one may develop an intense desire to obtain it. However, even the mere desire to obtain the item from another constitutes a transgression of the biblical prohibition not to covet that which belongs to your neighbor.

If the visitor uses persuasive pressure and thereby ultimately obtains the article, even through a legitimate sale, the prohibition is compounded. It may be common practice to engage in such negotiations, but the fact that it is common practice does not make it permissible.

Misconception: The biblical prohibition concerning weights is only that one may not use these false measurements.

It is surely prohibited to use false weights for measurement. However, the biblical law prohibits even maintaining such false weights in one's abode.

We are enjoined not only to refrain from doing that which is false but also to not have anything that is false.

19

Everyday Ethics

Misconception: Duplicating videos is acceptable practice.

In the videos that are available for purchase, there is usually a warning inserted at the beginning that forbids the individual from duplicating the video. In some instances, the duplicating is forbidden only for commercial purposes. In other instances, it is forbidden under any circumstances.

In all of these situations, the desires of the proprietor rule supreme. The producer of the video has the right to decide the conditions of duplication. If, in the interests of public education, a video producer allows duplication, there is no problem in making a copy. But if it is clearly stated in the video that duplicating it is prohibited, there is no allowance for doing so. The arguments that no one will know or that it is not fair for the video-producing company to make such restrictions are totally irrelevant.

Because it is the producer's property, the producer can decide how the item is to be used and how not to be used. These wishes must be respected. Anything less is theft.

Misconception: There is no prohibition against lifting material from someone's computer.

Theft from a computer is a new crime in this generation. It is also a most unique form of theft, because it is a situation in which in stealing from others, one takes away what belongs to the other, but the other still has what was stolen.

In a situation of stealing a computer program, for example, the program still remains, but now instead of there being just one program, there are two programs. This form of theft is likewise prohibited. The basic consideration that makes the taking of an item theft is that one takes what belongs to someone else against that other person's desire.

It is assumed that those who, for example, print programs and develop their own designs within their computer will share these only if they make this known. Otherwise, this is either available for purchase or considered secret until available.

Under these circumstances, taking away what belongs to others and what others do not want to share, even if this refusal is for selfish reasons, constitutes theft and is prohibited.

Misconception: There is no problem in extending an invitation to someone when you know the person will not accept.

This is a form of deceit and is forbidden. No rationale, such as the argument that it will engender good feelings, mitigates the severity of the breach.

This is not the same as extending invitations to out-of-town guests for an event, even though it may be clear the invitees cannot possibly attend. In such an instance, the invitation is sincere, and the inviters truly would like the guests to attend. But inviting others only because you know they cannot attend, and who would not be invited if they could attend, is emotional fraud.

Misconception: There is no religious objection to jaywalking.

If the law prohibits jaywalking, it is forbidden. The law of the land is the law and must be obeyed. Even if everyone else disobeys the law, that is no excuse.

If in fact jaywalking poses a danger, it would be further prohibited even in the absence of a local law prohibiting it, because it reflects dereliction of the responsibility to take care of oneself.

A devout Jew will not jaywalk.

Misconception: There is no Judaic prohibition associated with speeding.

It is obligatory to obey the law of the land. If the law of the land places a limitation upon the speed at which one may drive, one must abide by this regulation. To fail to do so is to renounce the basic Judaic responsibility to be an obedient citizen.

Even if there is no speed limit attached to specific roads, a certain amount of common sense must prevail. One must use one's intelligence to gauge what is a safe speed at which to drive.

Any speeding likely to cause an accident is likewise a contravention of Jewish law. The obligation to take care of oneself applies to all contingencies, including the force with which one presses down on the accelerator.

In addition, speeding involves danger to innocent others, who may be crippled or killed because a speeder lost control.

Misconception: There are no pollution-prevention laws in Judaism.

The potential for ecological damage caused by pollution is a by-product of the industrial revolution. More accurate scientific barometers of pollution's impact on the globe reveal that this is a serious, even critical, problem.

The importance of maintaining clean air was already recognized in talmudic times. It was a legally entrenched practice that a furnace that burned excess in any city had to be removed from the inhabited part of the city for health reasons.

On a scale that was appropriate to its time, there is much evidence of sensitivity to pollution in Judaic legal expression. This sensitivity must inform present Judaic practice regarding pollution prevention and control.

Misconception: Only the spouter of gossip transgresses.

Jewish law is categorical in its condemnation of gossip. It is considered a heinous crime, causing untold damage to the victim of the gossip in a most unfair way.

However, in every situation of gossip, there are three parties: the gossiper, the one about whom the gossip is being told, and the one listening to the gossip.

Were one to refuse to listen to gossip, there would be no gossip. Obviously, the drivel can be shared only if there is a spouter. But if there is no receiver, there will be no foul speech.

Because of this, the one who listens to the gossip is roundly condemned. By listening and giving credence to the gossiper, the receiver encourages the institution of bad-mouthing and becomes party to the insidious damage perpetrated on the person gossiped about. This is a biblical offense.

One should stay away from gossip in all its forms, including both transmitting and receiving.

Misconception: If the facts are true, one may publicly embarrass others.

This may be the case in secular law, whereby one is open to legal prosecution for libel only if the facts are untrue and therefore are liable as libel.

In Jewish law, one has no right to embarrass others, even if the facts are true. If the facts are not true, the embarrassment is a lie. A lie is forbidden, irrespective of whether or not it is the cause of embarrassment.

Even if statements are true, one may not publicly embarrass others. Our sensitivity to others dictates that we not shame them in public.

Misconception: One may share gossip with one's spouse.

Some tend to believe that saying evil about others applies as a prohibition only if it is spoken to others. Since husband and wife are as one, the sharing of gossip with one's spouse is effectively sharing it only with oneself. This should therefore entail no prohibition.

However, as much as husband and wife are perceived to be one, this principle does not apply to gossip. Insofar as gossip is concerned, even the husband and wife should not share and thereby spread the gossip. Gossiping is prohibited, even if husband or wife uses the logic that by sharing the gossip, one forges a closeness with one's mate.

Sharing in a pernicious way in order to build a relationship is using the most contemptible means to ostensibly build that which is most vital. By definition this cannot work.

Misconception: It is forbidden to talk too much with women.

There are some who mistakenly translate the famous statement in *Chapters of the Sages (Pirkay Avot)* as, "Do not engage in too much talk with women." This is a wrong translation with an attendant and unfortunately distorted conclusion.

The word that is used to describe conversation in this ethical statement is *sihah*, which is different from *dibur*. *Dibur* is speech and *sihah* is idle chatter or meaningless conversation.

In speaking meaningfully, in engaging in *dibur* with one's wife, one ennobles one's wife and places her on a solid and equal footing of respect within the marriage.

However, by seeing one's wife as merely the conduit for idle chatter about meaningless things, one diminishes one's wife and shows disrespect and even disdain for her. This is inexcusable and therefore is strongly discouraged.

Misconception: There are no limits to the amount of charity one may give.

Generally, we are all obliged to give 10 percent of our income to charity. Even a poor person is obliged to share in this manner.

However, there is also an upper limit for charity. One is not permitted to give away more than 20 percent of one's income during a calendar year.

The reason for this is that by overdoing one's charity commitment, one may become poor and then become a community charge. It is incongruous that by giving charity to help the poor, we should thereby encourage more poverty.

However, one may certainly give more than 20 percent of one's possessions to charity as a gift prior to one's passing from this world. Here the logic that one may become poor obviously does not apply.

Misconception: It is possible to be religious and miserly.

Religiosity and miserliness do not go together. In fact, they are antithetical.

An individual who is truly religious realizes that any bounty with which he or she is blessed is a gift from God. But God, Who bestowed the gift, has also asked that we share with others, either our families or those indigents who rely on individuals with means to help them through their poverty.

To neglect this profoundly religious responsibility by being miserly and holding on to one's money as if it were one's own is an act of sacrilegious proportions.

It must be fully appreciated that a miser cannot be a religious person, no matter how much the miser protests to the contrary. The religious spirit is at the same time a very generous spirit. A mean spirit is not a religious spirit.

There is no room for compromise on generosity of spirit.

Why 354?

This second volume contains 354 misconceptions. Why 354? For the 354 days of the year.

But, you ask, is not a year comprised of 365 days? That is a misconception! The solar year is 365 days. But the lunar year, which forms the basis of the Jewish calendar, is 354 days. A lunar month is about twenty-nine and a half days. Multiplied by twelve, this equals 354.

Enjoy this book every day of the (lunar) year.

Sources

Chapter 1   Setting the Record Straight

page

3   Genesis 3:12. See also Reuven P. Bulka, *What You Thought You Knew about Judaism: 341 Common Misconceptions about Jewish Life* (Northvale, NJ: Jason Aronson Inc., 1989), pp. 348–349.

4   *Rashi* to Genesis 6:3.

5   Genesis 7:2.

6   *Rashi* to Genesis 29:13; Ibn Ezra to Genesis 25:34.

7   See Reuven P. Bulka, "The Selling of the Birthright: Making Sense of a Perplexing Episode," *The Jewish Bible Quarterly: Dor LeDor* 19:2 (1990–1991): 100–104.

8   See Genesis 25:34. See also Reuven P. Bulka, "Isaac's Blessing— Who Was Deceived?" *Dor LeDor: Our Biblical Heritage* 17: 3 (1989): 185–189.

9   See *Rashi* to Genesis 29:28.

10   See Yehudah Nachshoni, *Hagut BeParshiyot HaTorah* (Bnay Brak, 1979), p. 174.

11   *Bava Metzia* 87a.

12   See Exodus 12:16. See also Rabbi Meir Simhah of Dvinsk, *Meshekh Hokhmah* (Jerusalem: Eshkol, n. d.), on that verse.

13–14   See Genesis 15:13. See also, for example, Deuteronomy 10:19.

15   See Exodus 12:51.

16   See *Sanhedrin* 56b.

17   Exodus 20:13; *Sanhedrin* 72a.

18   See *Zevahim* 116a.

19   See Exodus 31:1–11.

20   See Exodus 33:11; Numbers 27:18; *Bava Batra* 75a.

21   Compare Genesis 23:7 with *Avot* 2:6.

22   See Jacov Even-Chen, *Rabbi Joseph Karo Life Story* (Jerusalem: HaKtav Institute, 1988).

23   *Encyclopaedia Judaica*, vol. 5 (Jerusalem: Keter Publishing House, 1971), pp. 195–198.

24   Ibid., vol. 11, pp. 1178–1211.

25   See, for example, Yaffa Eliach, *Hasidic Tales of the Holocaust* (New York: Oxford University Press, 1982).

Chapter 2   About This and That

page
29   Deuteronomy 10:20.
30   See *TaZ* to *Shulhan Arukh, Orah Hayyim* 621:4 n. 2.
31   See, for example, *Avot* 2:1.
32   See Aharon of Barcelona, *Sefer HaHinukh* (Israel: Eshkol, 1965).
33   See Reuven P. Bulka, "Love Your Neighbor: Halachic Parameters," *Journal of Halacha and Contemporary Society* 16 (1988): 44–54.
34   See *Shulhan Arukh, Yoreh De'ah* 283:4, and *TaZ* n. 3.
35   See Leviticus 1:1–7:38.
36   See Samson Raphael Hirsch, *The Pentateuch: Translated and Explained*, vol. 3, *Leviticus, Part 1 (London: L. Honig and Sons, 1962), pp. 6–7.*
37–38   *Gittin* 60b.
39   See Rabbi Eliezer Papo, *Pele Yo'etz* (Jerusalem, 1987), pp. 23–24, under category of *avelut*.
40   *Sanhedrin* 97b.
41   See *Shabbat* 133b.
42   See *Shulhan Arukh, Orah Hayyim* 128:40.
43   See *Berakhot* 34b, and commentary of Etz Yosef in *Ayn Yaakov*, vol. 1 (New York: Pardes, n. d.), p. 139.
44   See *Shulhan Arukh, Yoreh De'ah* 157:1.
45   See *Shabbat* 138b.
46   See Rabbi Yehiel Mikhel Tukacinsky, *Gesher HaHayyim*, vol. 1 (Jerusalem: Solomon Press, 1960), pp. 143–145.
47   See *Avot* 1:17, 2:5.
48   See *Avot* 1:12.
49   Papo, *Pele Yo'etz*, p. 364, under category of *levishah*.

Chapter 3   Tallit, Tefillin, Mezuzah, and Kipah

page
53   See *Shulhan Arukh, Orah Hayyim* 4:1, and *Mishnah Berurah*, loc. cit. n. 1.
54   Rabbi Yosef Eliyahu Henkin, *Eydut LeYisrael* (New York: Walden Press n. d.), p. 114.
55   See *Shulhan Arukh, Orah Hayyim* 8:2, 10:1.
56   *Shulhan Arukh, Orah Hayyim* 8:14; see also *Mishnah Berurah*, loc. cit. n. 37.
57   See *Shulhan Arukh, Orah Hayyim* 8:2.

page
58 See Rabbi Yonah Metzger, *MeYam HaHalakhah*, vol. 1 (Tel Aviv, 1988), p. 37.
59 See *Shulhan Arukh, Orah Hayyim* 24:1; *Mishnah Berurah* to *Shulhan Arukh, Orah Hayyim* 58:1 n. 5.
60 *Shulhan Arukh, Orah Hayyim* 11:1.
61 *Shulhan Arukh, Orah Hayyim* 9:5; *Mishnah Berurah*, loc. cit. n. 15, 16.
62 See *Mishnah Berurah* to *Shulhan Arukh, Orah Hayyim* 15:2 n. 6.
63 *Shulhan Arukh, Orah Hayyim* 23:1.
64 See *Mishnah Berurah* to *Shulhan Arukh, Orah Hayyim* 58:1 n. 5.
65 *Shulhan Arukh, Orah Hayyim* 27:6.
66 *Shulhan Arukh, Orah Hayyim* 42:1.
67 See *Shulhan Arukh, Orah Hayyim* 32:40.
68 *Shulhan Arukh, Orah Hayyim* 33:3.
69 See *Shulhan Arukh, Orah Hayyim* 565:5, 581:1, 30:1-3.
70 *Shulhan Arukh, Yoreh De'ah* 285:1-2.
71 *Shulhan Arukh, Yoreh De'ah* 286:22.
72 *Shulhan Arukh, Yoreh De'ah* 285:1.
73 *Shulhan Arukh, Yoreh De'ah* 291:2.
74 *Shulhan Arukh, Yoreh De'ah* 291:2.
75 See *Shulhan Arukh, Orah Hayyim* 91:4.
76 See *Mishnah Berurah* to *Shulhan Arukh, Orah Hayyim* 2:6 n. 11, 12.

Chapter 4 *Prayer*

page
79 See Rabbi Gedalyah Felder, *Yesoday Yeshurun*, vol. 1 (New York: J. Biegeleisen, 1977), pp. 28-29.
80 See Rabbi Dr. Joseph B. Soloveitchik, "Seating and Sanctification," in Baruch Litvin, ed., *The Sanctity of the Synagogue* (New York: Spero Foundation, 1959), pp. 114-118.
81 See *Shulhan Arukh, Orah Hayyim* 96:1.
82 See *Shulhan Arukh, Orah Hayyim* 93:3.
83 See Rabbi Gedalyah Felder, *Yesoday Yeshurun*, vol. 1 (New York: J. Biegeleisen, 1977), pp. 1-2.
84 *Shulhan Arukh, Orah Hayyim* 101:2; see *Mishnah Berurah*, loc. cit. n. 6.
85 *Shulhan Arukh, Orah Hayyim* 124:12.
86 See *Shulhan Arukh, Orah Hayyim* 48:1, and *Magen Avraham*, loc. cit. n. 4.
87 See *Shulhan Arukh, Orah Hayyim* 128:33.
88 See *Mishnah Berurah* to *Shulhan Arukh, Orah Hayyim* 128:33 n. 120.

page
89 *Shulhan Arukh, Orah Hayyim* 92:1.
90 *Shulhan Arukh, Orah Hayyim* 108:1-3.
91 *Shulhan Arukh, Orah Hayyim* 108:6.
92 *Shulhan Arukh, Orah Hayyim* 108:4.
93 See *Shulhan Arukh, Orah Hayyim* 61:5.
94 *Shulhan Arukh, Orah Hayyim* 65:2-3. See also *Mishnah Berurah*, loc. cit. n. 11.
95 See *Biur Halakhah* to *Mishnah Berurah, Orah Hayyim* 426:4, last note, starting with the word *velo*.
96 Abraham Sperling, *Taamay HaMinhagim U'Mekoray HaDinim* (Jerusalem: Eshkol, n. d.), p. 37 n. 66.
97 See Rabbi Dr. Joseph Hertz, *The Authorized Daily Prayer Book* (New York: Bloch Publishing Company, 1974), p. 529.
98 See, for example, *Shulhan Arukh, Orah Hayyim* 282:1, 137:1.
99 *Shulhan Arukh, Orah Hayyim* 69:1.
100 See *Shulhan Arukh, Orah Hayyim* 55:2-3.
101 See *Mishnah Berurah* to *Shulhan Arukh, Orah Hayyim* 90:9 n. 28.
102 See *Encyclopaedia Judaica,* vol. 7 (Jerusalem: Keter Publishing House, 1971), pp. 1542-1544.
103 See *Mishnah Berurah* to *Shulhan Arukh, Orah Hayyim* 146: 4 n. 17, and *Shaar HaZiyun*, loc. cit. n. 18, that even standing when the ark is open is not mandatory.
104 See Dovid Zucker and Rabbi Moshe Francis, *Chol HaMoed: Comprehensive Review of the Laws of the Intermediate Days of the Festivals* (Lakewood, NJ: Halacha Publications, 1981), p. 118 n. 6. See also *Shulhan Arukh, Orah Hayyim* 236:2; Shlomoh Tal, *Siddur Rinat Yisrael* (Jerusalem: Morashah Publishing, 1977), p. 165.
105 *Shulhan Arukh, Orah Hayyim* 117:1.

Chapter 5   Torah Matters

page
109 Exodus 24:7.
110 See *Shulhan Arukh, Yoreh De'ah* 281:1.
111 *Shulhan Arukh, Yoreh De'ah* 282:9.
112 See *Shulhan Arukh, Yoreh De'ah* 282:2.
113 *Shulhan Arukh, Orah Hayyim* 135:12.
114 See *Shulhan Arukh, Orah Hayyim* 128:40.
115 See Rabbi Gedalyah Felder, *Yesoday Yeshurun*, vol. 1 (New York: J. Biegeleisen, 1977), p. 250.
116 *Shulhan Arukh, Orah Hayyim* 141:6, and *Mishnah Berurah*, loc. cit. n. 18.

Sources 409

page
117 See *Mishnah Berurah* to *Shulhan Arukh*, *Orah Hayyim* 141:6 n. 20, 21.
118 *Shulhan Arukh*, *Orah Hayyim* 141:7.
119 See *Mishnah Berurah* to *Shulhan Arukh*, *Orah Hayyim* 134:2 n. 8. See also Rabbi Shlomoh Ganzfried, *Kitzur Shulhan Arukh* (Tel Aviv: Sinai, 1974), 23:25.
120 *Shulhan Arukh*, *Orah Hayyim* 134:2.
121 *Shulhan Arukh*, *Orah Hayyim* 144:2.
122 *Shulhan Arukh*, *Orah Hayyim* 685:1, and *Mishnah Berurah*, loc. cit. n. 5.

Chapter 6   Blessings

page
125 *Shulhan Arukh*, *Orah Hayyim* 210:1.
126 *Shulhan Arukh*, *Orah Hayyim* 177:1, and *Mishnah Berurah*, loc. cit. n. 3.
127 *Shulhan Arukh*, *Orah Hayyim* 175.
128 *Shulhan Arukh*, *Orah Hayyim* 202:1.
129 *Shulhan Arukh*, *Orah Hayyim* 208:10.
130 *Berakhot* 46a; *Shulhan Arukh*, *Orah Hayyim* 201:1.
131 *Shulhan Arukh*, *Orah Hayyim* 190:1.
132 See the excellent work by Rabbi Abner Weiss, *Death and Bereavement: A Halakhic Guide* (Hoboken, NJ: Ktav Publishing House; New York: Union of Orthodox Jewish Congregations of America, 1991), pp. 269–279.
133 *Megillah* 21b.
134 *Shulhan Arukh*, *Orah Hayyim* 128:39; *Mishnah Berurah*, loc. cit. n. 144–146.
135 *Shulhan Arukh*, *Orah Hayyim* 128:26; *Mishnah Berurah*, loc. cit. n. 102, 103.
136 *Shulhan Arukh*, *Orah Hayyim* 128:44; *Mishnah Berurah*, loc. cit. n. 164.
137 *Shulhan Arukh*, *Orah Hayyim* 219:1-2, 8. See also Rabbi Shlomoh Aviner, *Am K'Lavi* (Jerusalem, 1983), pp. 66–67.
138 *Shulhan Arukh*, *Orah Hayyim* 426:4; *Mishnah Berurah*, loc. cit. n. 21.

Chapter 7   Kosher Tidbits

page
141 Emily Soloff, "A Muslim Hekhsher," *The Jerusalem Report*, January 17, 1991, pp. 27–29.
142 See the discussion by Dayan I. Grunfeld, *The Jewish Dietary Laws*, vol. 1 (London: Soncino Press, 1972), pp. 3–25.

page
143   See E. Eidlitz, *Is It Kosher? Encyclopedia of Kosher Food Facts and Fallacies* (Jerusalem and New York: Feldheim Publishers, 1992), pp. 139–140.
144   *Shulhan Arukh, Orah Hayyim* 181:1, 181:10.
145   See, for example, Exodus 23:19. See also Grunfeld, *Jewish Dietary Laws*, pp. 115–139.
146   *Shulhan Arukh, Yoreh De'ah* 89:2.
147   *Shulhan Arukh, Yoreh De'ah* 87:3.
148   *Shulhan Arukh, Yoreh De'ah* 97:1.
149   See Rabbi Hayyim David HaLevi, *Aseh Lekha Rav*, vol. 5 (Tel Aviv, 1983), p. 344, no. 31.
150   *Shulhan Arukh, Yoreh De'ah* 85:1.
151   *Shulhan Arukh, Yoreh De'ah* 66:10.
152   *Shulhan Arukh, Yoreh De'ah* 83:1.
153   Numbers 15:20. See Rabbi Aharon of Barcelona, *Sefer HaHinukh* (Israel: Eshkol, 1965), pp. 227–228, *mitzvah* 385.
154   *Shulhan Arukh, Yoreh De'ah* 120:1.
155   *Shulhan Arukh, Yorah De'ah* 120:1.
156   Deuteronomy 20:19–20. See Rabbi Aharon of Barcelona, *Sefer HaHinukh*, pp. 319–320, *mitzvah* 529.
157   *Magen Avraham* to *Shulhan Arukh, Orah Hayyim* 167:6 n. 18.
158   See Leo Landman, ed., *Judaism and Drugs* (New York: Commission on Synagogue Relations of Federation of Jewish Philanthropies of New York, 1973).

Chapter 8   Shabbat

page
161   *Shulhan Arukh, Orah Hayyim* 263:2–3.
162   *Shulhan Arukh, Orah Hayyim* 263:3.
163   Rabbi Eliezer Papo, *Pele Yo'etz* (Jerusalem, 1987), p. 54, under category of *berakhot*.
164   *Shulhan Arukh, Orah Hayyim* 288:4.
165   *Shulhan Arukh, Orah Hayyim* 308.
166   See *Mishnah Berurah* to *Shulhan Arukh, Orah Hayyim* 308:41 n. 153.
167   *Shulhan Arukh, Orah Hayyim* 277.
168   Exodus 20:8.
169   See Rabbi Aryeh Ginzberg, *Divray Hakhamim* (Brooklyn, NY: Rabbi Z. Berman Books, 1986), p. 100, no. 277.
170   *Shulhan Arukh, Yoreh De'ah* 400:1.

page
171 See, for example, Numbers 28:9–10. See also *Eruvin* 103a.
172 See *Mishnah Berurah* to *Shulhan Arukh, Orah Hayyim* 284:3 n. 6.
173 See *Mishnah Berurah* to *Shulhan Arukh, Orah Hayyim* 284:1 n. 2.
174 See Rabbi Dr. Joseph Hertz, *The Authorized Daily Prayer Book* (New York: Bloch Publishing Company, 1974), p. 749. Rabbi Nosson Scherman, *The Complete ArtScroll Siddur* (Brooklyn, NY: Mesorah Publications, 1984), pp. 620–621, translates *hol* as "secular."
175 *Shulhan Arukh, Orah Hayyim* 299:6.
176 *Shulhan Arukh, Orah Hayyim* 299:6.
177 *Shulhan Arukh, Orah Hayyim* 297:1, 298:1.
178 *Shulhan Arukh, Orah Hayyim* 298:1.

Chapter 9   Festivals and Special Days

page
181 See *Mishnah Berurah* to *Shulhan Arukh, Orah Hayyim* 494:1 n. 1.
182 See *Shulhan Arukh, Orah Hayyim* 472:1. See also *Mishnah Berurah* to *Shulhan Arukh, Orah Hayyim* 261:2 n. 19.
183 See *Mishnah Berurah* to *Shulhan Arukh, Orah Hayyim* 471:2 n. 16. See also *Shulhan Arukh, Orah Hayyim* 529:1, 249:2.
184 *Shulhan Arukh, Orah Hayyim* 446:1. See also *Mishnah Berurah* to *Shulhan Arukh, Orah Hayyim* 435:1 n. 5.
185 *Mishneh Torah, Laws of the Festivals* 6:17–18; *Shulhan Arukh, Orah Hayyim* 529:2.
186 *Shulhan Arukh, Orah Hayyim* 546:2.
187 See *Shulhan Arukh, Orah Hayyim* 651:15.
188 See *Shulhan Arukh, Orah Hayyim* 669:1, 668:2.
189 See *Shulhan Arukh, Orah Hayyim* 665:8. See *Mishnah Berurah* to *Shulhan Arukh, Orah Hayyim* 445:1 n. 7.
190 *Shulhan Arukh, Orah Hayyim* 527:13.
191 See *Mishnah Berurah* to *Shulhan Arukh, Orah Hayyim* 527:1 n. 3.
192 See Reuven P. Bulka, *Torah Therapy: Reflections on the Weekly Sedra and Special Occasions* (New York: Ktav Publishing House, 1983), pp. 137–139.
193 Rabbi Shlomoh Ganzfried, *Kitzur Shulhan Arukh* (Tel Aviv: Sinai Publishing 1974), 128:2.
194 *Shulhan Arukh, Orah Hayyim* 582:9. See *Mishnah Berurah*, loc. cit. n. 25, about whether one should invoke *veTayhataymu* or *veTayhataymi*.
195 See Rabbi Shlomoh Zevin, *HaMoadim beHalakhah* (Tel Aviv: A. Zioni, 1959), pp. 48–53.

page
196   See *Shulhan Arukh, Orah Hayyim* 583:2, and *Mishnah Berurah*, loc. cit.
      n. 9. Regarding the mazal statement, Rabbi Yehiel Mikhel Epstein,
      Arukh HaShulhan, vol. 3 (New York: E. Grossman, n. d.), *Orah
      Hayyim* 597:2, states that he could not find the text, supposedly in the
      Jerusalem Talmud.
197   See *Shulhan Arukh, Orah Hayyim* 605:1.
198   See *Encyclopaedia Judaica*, vol. 10 (Jerusalem: Keter Publishing
      House, 1971), pp. 1166–1167.
199   *Taanit* 26b. See also *Shulhan Arukh, Orah Hayyim* 610.
200   See *Mishnah Berurah* to *Shulhan Arukh, Orah Hayyim* 670:1 n. 1.
201   *Shulhan Arukh, Orah Hayyim* 671:7.
202   See *Mishnah Berurah* to *Shulhan Arukh, Orah Hayyim* 670:1 n. 1.
203   See Rabbi Shlomoh Aviner, *Am keLavi* (Jerusalem, 1983), p. 179, no.
      214.
204   *Shulhan Arukh, Orah Hayyim* 676:1.
205   See *Shulhan Arukh, Orah Hayyim* 679, and *Mishnah Berurah*, loc. cit. n.
      2.
206   See the interesting piece by Meir Greenwald, "*HaSevivon veSevivato.*"
      In *Sefer HaMoadim*, vol. 5 (Rosh Hodesh, Hanukah, 15th of Shevat)
      (Tel Aviv: Dvir, 1977), pp. 225–226.
207   See *Biur Halakhah* to *Shulhan Arukh, Orah Hayyim* 670:2, beginning
      with the word *venohagin*.
208   *Shulhan Arukh, Orah Hayyim* 677:4. See also Rabbi Shlomoh Ganz-
      fried, *Kitzur Shulhan Arukh* (Tel Aviv: Sinai Publishing, 1974),
      139:20.
209   See *Shulhan Arukh, Orah Hayyim* 694:1, and *Mishnah Berurah,* loc. cit.
      n. 3.
210   See *Shulhan Arukh, Orah Hayyim*, 694:1, and *Mishnah Berurah*, loc. cit.
      n. 1. See also *Shulhan Arukh, Orah Hayyim* 689:1.
211   See *Shulhan Arukh, Orah Hayyim* 427.
212   See *Shulhan Arukh, Orah Hayyim* 426:3.
213   See *Mishnah Berurah* to *Shulhan Arukh, Orah Hayyim* 426:4 n. 20.
214   See Rabbi Ralph Pelcovitz, "Reciting the Hallel on Yom Haatz-
      maut," *Journal of Halacha and Contemporary Society* 7 (1984): 5–18.

Chapter 10   *Not-So-Happy Days*

page
217   Leviticus 23:15–22; *Shulhan Arukh, Orah Hayyim* 493:1–4.
218   See Rabbi Aryeh Ginzberg, *Divray Hakhamim* (Brooklyn, NY: Rabbi
      Z. Berman Books, 1986), pp. 148–149, no. 420.

page
219   Ibid., p. 149, no. 421.
220   *Shulhan Arukh, Orah Hayyim* 493:1.
221   *Shulhan Arukh, Orah Hayyim* 489:4.
222   *Shulhan Arukh, Orah Hayyim* 493:2.
223   *Shulhan Arukh, Orah Hayyim* 493:2; *Mishnah Berurah* to *Shulhan Arukh, Orah Hayyim* 260:1 n. 5.
224   See *Shulhan Arukh, Orah Hayyim* 551:1-18.
225   Ginzberg, *Divray Hakhamim*, p. 163, no. 462.
226   See Rabbi Ovadyah Yosef, *Yehaveh Daat*, vol. 1 (Jerusalem: A. B. Printing, 1977), pp. 103-105, no. 36. See also *Shulhan Arukh, Orah Hayyim* 551:2.
227   *Mishnah Berurah* to *Shulhan Arukh, Orah Hayyim* 551:15 n. 87; *Shaaray Teshuvah* to *Shulhan Arukh, Orah Hayyim* 551:1 n. 3.
228   See, for example, Ginzberg, *Divray Hakhamim*, pp. 162-163, no. 461.
229   See *Shulhan Arukh, Orah Hayyim* 555:22.
230   See *Shulhan Arukh, Orah Hayyim* 559:4; *Berakhot* 2:4.
231   See *Mishnah Berurah* to *Shulhan Arukh, Orah Hayyim* 554:18 n. 37.
232   *Shulhan Arukh, Orah Hayyim* 614:2, 554:16.
233   See *Shulhan Arukh, Orah Hayyim* 568:12.
234   See *Shulhan Arukh, Orah Hayyim* 618. See also *Mishnah Berurah* to *Shulhan Arukh, Orah Hayyim* 550:1 n. 4.
235   Rabbi Shlomoh Ganzfried, *Kitzur Shulhan Arukh* (Tel Aviv: Sinai Publishing, 1974), 121:9.
236   *Shulhan Arukh, Orah Hayyim* 565:3.

Chapter 11   *Marriage*

page
239   See *Biur Halakhah* to *Shulhan Arukh, Orah Hayyim* 136, item beginning with the word *BeShabbat*.
240   Ibid.
241   See Rabbi Shalom Mordekhai HaKohen Schwadron, *Responsa of MaHaRSHaM*, vol. 3 (Jerusalem: Makhon Hatam Sofer, 1974), pp. 91b-92a, no. 136.
242   Rabbi Mosheh Shternbuch, *Teshuvot veHanhagot* (Jerusalem: Netivot HaTorah V'haHesed, 1986), pp. 262-263, no. 756.
243   Shternbuch, *Teshuvot veHanhagot*, p. 258, no. 743.
244   See *Shulhan Arukh, Even HaEzer* 28:1, 28:19. See also Rabbi Yehiel Mikhel Epstein, *Arukh HaShulhan*, vol. 6 (New York: E. Grossman, n.d.), *Even HaEzer* 28:84.

page
245 See *Shulhan Arukh, Even HaEzer* 64:4. See also *Pit'hay Teshuvah* to *Shulhan Arukh, Even HaEzer* 64:4, no. 4.
246 Binyamin Adler, *HaNisuin keHilkhatam* (Jerusalem: HaMesorah, 1984), p. 167, no. 9.
247 See *Bet Shmuel* to *Shulhan Arukh, Even HaEzer* 62:4 n. 4.
248 Adler, *HaNisuin keHilkhatam*, pp. 273–274.
249 See *Helkat Mehokek* to *Shulhan Arukh, Even HaEzer* 62:4 n. 3.
250 *Shulhan Arukh, Even HaEzer* 62:5.
251 See Reuven P. Bulka, "Love Your Neighbor: Halachic Parameters," *Journal of Halacha and Contemporary Society* 16 (1988): 44–54.
252 Rabbi Mosheh Feinstein, *Igrot Mosheh* to *Yoreh De'ah*, vol. 3 (Bnay Brak: Yeshivat Ohel Yosef, 1981), pp. 309–310, no. 60.
253 See Reuven P. Bulka, *Jewish Marriage: A Halakhic Ethic* (Hoboken, NJ: Ktav Publishing House; New York: Yeshiva University Press, 1986), pp. 124–125.
254 See *Shulhan Arukh, Orah Hayyim* 2:1–2.
255 See *Shulhan Arukh, Even HaEzer* 119:6.
256 See *Shulhan Arukh, Even HaEzer* 66:3.

Chapter 12   *Divorce*

page
259 See, for example, *Ketuvot* 61b.
260 See, for example, *Encyclopaedia Judaica*, vol. 6 (Jerusalem: Keter Publishing House, 1971), p. 135.
261 See *Shulhan Arukh, Even HaEzer* 6:1, 10:3.
262 Rabbi Aharon of Barcelona, *Sefer HaHinukh* (Israel: Eshkol Press, 1965), pp. 344–347, *mitzvah* no. 579.
263 See Reuven P. Bulka, *Jewish Divorce Ethics: The Right Way to Say Goodbye* (Ogdensburg, NY: Ivy League Press, 1992).
264 Ibid., p. 152.
265 See *Shulhan Arukh, Even HaEzer* 178:18.
266 See *Shulhan Arukh, Even HaEzer* 154:1.
267 *Shulhan Arukh, Even HaEzer* 154:1.
268 See *Bet Shmuel* to *Shulhan Arukh, Even HaEzer* 154:1 n. 2. The extent of the "right" to a *get* is a matter of debate.
269 Bulka, *Jewish Divorce Ethics*, pp. 159–160.
270 Ibid., p. 28.
271 See Exodus 23:7; *Shavuot* 31a.
272 Bulka, *Jewish Divorce Ethics*, pp. 230–236.

page
273 See 1 Kings 3:16-27.
274 See Bulka, *Jewish Divorce Ethics*, pp. 194-229.
275 Ibid., pp. 211-212.
276 Ibid., pp. 213-215.
277 Ibid., pp. 212-213.

Chapter 13   Parents and Children

page
281 *Shulhan Arukh, Even HaEzer* 4:13.
282 Deuteronomy 23:3; *Horayot* 13a.
283 Ecclesiastes 13:24.
284 Leviticus 19:3.
285 Deuteronomy 24:16; Exodus 34:7; *Berakhot* 7a.
286-287 *Shulhan Arukh, Yoreh De'ah* 240:17.
288 Numbers 27:5-11. See also *Shulhan Arukh, Hoshen Mishpat* 281:1, 7.
289 Rabbi Yekutiel Yehudah Greenwald, *Kol Bo al Avelut* (New York: Feldheim, 1965), pp. 53-54.
290 *Shulhan Arukh, Yoreh De'ah* 240:24, 4.

Chapter 14   New Homes, New Children

page
293 Genesis 1:10, 12.
294 *Shulhan Arukh, Orah Hayyim* 223:3; *Mishnah Berurah*, loc. cit. n. 11, 12.
295 See Rabbi Yosef David Weissberg, *Sefer Otzar HaBrit*, vol. 1 (Jerusalem: Machon Torat HaBrit, 1986), p. 226, no. 1.
296 Ibid., pp. 222, no. 1.
297 Asher Anshil Greenwald, *Zokher HaBrit* (Israel, 1964), p. 146, no. 20.
298 See Reuven P. Bulka, *The Jewish Pleasure Principle* (New York: Human Sciences Press, 1989), pp. 46-47.
299 See *Mishneh Torah, Laws of Circumcision* 2:2.
300 See *RCA Orthodox Roundtable: Opinion Concerning Metzitzah & AIDS*. Available from RCA Roundtable, 5625 Arlington Avenue, Riverdale, New York 10471.
301 *Shulhan Arukh, Yoreh De'ah* 305:18.
302 *Shulhan Arukh, Yoreh De'ah* 305:3.
303 See *SHaKH* to *Shulhan Arukh, Yoreh De'ah* 305:10 n. 11. See also *Pit'hay Teshuvah*, loc. cit. n. 17.
304 *Shulhan Arukh, Yoreh De'ah* 305:10.

page
305 See *Mishnah Berurah* to *Shulhan Arukh, Orah Hayyim* 128:6 n. 22.
306 *Shulhan Arukh, Yoreh De'ah* 268:7. See Rabbi Gedalyah Felder, *Nahalat Zvi*, vol. 1 (New York, 1978), pp. 25–28.
307 See *Shabbat* 89b.

Chapter 15   Confronting Mortality

page
311 See Reuven P. Bulka, *Critical Psychological Issues: Judaic Perspectives* (Lanham, MD: University Press of America, 1992), pp. 103–126.
312 See Jerusalem Talmud, *Shabbat* 14:3. See also Reuven P. Bulka, *The Jewish Pleasure Principle* (New York: Human Sciences Press, 1989), pp. 31–33. 275. *Shulhan Arukh, Yoreh De'ah* 335:4.
313 *Shulhan Arukh, Yoreh De'ah* 335:4.
314 *Shulhan Arukh, Yoreh De'ah* 339:3.
315 See *TaZ* to *Shulhan Arukh, Yoreh De'ah* 340:12 n. 6.
316 *Shulhan Arukh, Yoreh De'ah* 340:9.
317 See, for example, *Shulhan Arukh, Yoreh De'ah* 340:9; Rabbi Yekutiel Yehudah Greenwald, *Kol Bo al Avelut* (New York: Feldheim, 1965), p. 28 n. 8.
318 *Shulhan Arukh, Yoreh De'ah* 340:14.
319 *Shulhan Arukh, Yoreh De'ah* 340:31.
320 Greenwald, *Kol Bo al Avelut*, p. 269.
321 See *Shulhan Arukh, Yoreh De'ah* 340:9; Greenwald, *Kol Bo al Avelut*, p. 29 n. 10; Rabbi Yehiel Mikhel Tukacinsky, *Gesher HaHayyim*, vol. 1 (Jerusalem: Solomon Press, 1960), p. 213.
322 See *Shulhan Arukh, Yoreh De'ah* 357:1; Greenwald, *Kol Bo al Avelut*, p. 39 n. 12.
323 *Shulhan Arukh, Yoreh De'ah* 373:4.
324 *Shulhan Arukh, Yoreh De'ah* 344:1; Rabbi Gedalyah Felder, *Yesoday Yeshurun*, vol. 6 (New York: Balshon, 1970), p. 31.
325 See *Shulhan Arukh, Yoreh De'ah* 344:16, 17; *TaZ*, 344:17 n. 5.
326 See Tukacinsky, *Gesher HaHayyim*, pp. 148–149.

Chapter 16   Mourning

page
329 *Shulhan Arukh, Yoreh De'ah* 378:1. Rabbi Yekutiel Yehudah Greenwald, *Kol Bo al Avelut* (New York: Feldheim, 1965), p. 272.
330 Rabbi Yehiel Mikhel Tukacinsky, *Gesher HaHayyim*, vol. 1 (Jerusalem: Solomon Press, 1960), p. 200.

page
331   Ibid., p. 181.
332   See *Shulhan Arukh, Yoreh De'ah* 375:2.
333   *Shulhan Arukh, Yoreh De'ah* 375:8.
334   See Rabbi Aaron Felder, *Yesodei Smochos* (New York, 1976), p. 81 n. 4a.
335   See *Shulhan Arukh, Yoreh De'ah* 387:1-2, and *SHaKH*, loc. cit. n. 1.
336   *Shulhan Arukh, Orah Hayyim* 548:6.
337   *Shulhan Arukh, Yoreh De'ah* 375:7.
338   On sensitivity regarding what one says to the mourner, see *Shulhan Arukh, Yoreh De'ah* 376:1-2.
339   See Rabbi Yehiel Mikhel Epstein, *Arukh HaShulhan*, vol. 5 (New York: E. Grossman Publishing House n.d.), *Yoreh De'ah* 343:4.
340   See, for example, Greenwald, *Kol Bo al Avelut*, pp. 297-298.
341   *Shulhan Arukh, Yoreh De'ah* 387:1, and *SHaKH* to 387:2 n. 1.
342   *Shulhan Arukh, Orah Hayyim* 696:6, and *Mishnah Berurah*, loc. cit., nos. 19-21. See also Felder, *Yesodei Smochos*, p. 87.
343   *Shulhan Arukh, Yoreh De'ah* 392:1.
344   See Greenwald, *Kol Bo al Avelut*, p. 336 n. 3.
345   See *Shulhan Arukh, Orah Hayyim* 559:6.
346   See *Sha'aray Teshuvah* to *Shulhan Arukh, Orah Hayyim* 554:1 n. 1.

Chapter 17   *Mourning After Mourning*

page
349   *Shulhan Arukh, Yoreh De'ah* 385:1.
350   Rabbi Yehiel Mikhel Tukacinsky, *Gesher HaHayyim*, vol. 1 (Jerusalem: Solomon Press 1960), pp. 276-277.
351   *Shulhan Arukh, Yoreh De'ah* 403:1-2.
352   See Rabbi Eliezer Papo, *Pele Yo'etz* (Jerusalem, 1987), pp. 36-37, under category of *Amen*.
353   Rabbi Yekutiel Yehudah Greenwald, *Kol Bo al Avelut* (New York: Feldheim, 1965), p. 375 n. 33.
354   See *Shulhan Arukh, Yoreh De'ah* 391:2.
355   *Shulhan Arukh, Yoreh De'ah* 364:1, and *SHaKH*, loc. cit. n. 3.
356   See Rabbi Aaron Felder, *Yesodei Smochos* (New York, 1976), p. 126.
357   See Rabbi Avraham Yitzhak Sperling, *Taamay HaMinhagim uMekoray HaDinim* (Jerusalem: Eshkol, n.d.), pp. 470-471, no. 1069.
358   *Shulhan Arukh, Yoreh De'ah* 402:12; Greenwald, *Kol Bo al Avelut*, pp. 388-389.
359   Greenwald, *Kol Bo al Avelut*, p. 388 n. 2.
360   Ibid., p. 394; Tukacinsky, *Gesher HaHayyim*, p. 346.

page
361   Rabbis Yeshayahu Aryeh and Yehoshua Dvorkes, *Siddur Minhat Yerushalayim: Kol Bo Hashalem* (Jerusalem, 1977), p. 668.

Chapter 18   Business Ethics

page
365   See, for example, *Encyclopaedia Judaica*, vol. 4 (Jerusalem: Keter Publishing House, 1971), p. 719.
366   *Shulhan Arukh, Hoshen Mishpat* 26:1.
367   *Shulhan Arukh, Hoshen Mishpat* 235:22, 20; *Eruvin* 65a.
368   *Shulhan Arukh, Hoshen Mishpat* 421:4.
369   *Shulhan Arukh, Hoshen Mishpat* 422:1.
370   *Shulhan Arukh, Yoreh De'ah* 175:1, 4.
371   *Shulhan Arukh, Hoshen Mishpat* 228:6. See also *Me'irat Aynayim*, loc. cit. n. 7.
372   Rabbi Yehiel Mikhel Epstein, *Arukh HaShulhan*, vol. 8 (New York: E. Grossman, n.d.), *Hoshen Mishpat* 227:1.
373   *Shulhan Arukh, Hoshen Mishpat* 227:1.
374   Epstein, *Arukh HaShulhan, Hoshen Mishpat* 227:1.
375   *Shulhan Arukh, Hoshen Mishpat* 333:3; *SHaKH*, loc. cit. n. 14.
376   *Shulhan Arukh, Hoshen Mishpat* 337:19.
377   *Shulhan Arukh, Yoreh De'ah* 162:1.
378   *Shulhan Arukh, Yoreh De'ah* 177:14.
379   Rabbi S. Wagschal, *Torah Guide for the Businessman* (Jerusalem: Feldheim, 1990), p. 172.
380   *Shulhan Arukh, Yoreh De'ah* 163:1.335. *Shulhan Arukh, Yoreh De'ah* 163:1.
381   *Shulhan Arukh, Yoreh De'ah* 160:21.
382   See Wagschal, *Torah Guide for the Businessman*, p. 180.
383   See *Shulhan Arukh, Orah Hayyim* 170:13.
384   See Wagschal, *Torah Guide for the Businessman*, pp. 141–142.
385   Rabbi Yisrael Meir HaKohen, *Sefer Hafetz Hayyim* (New York: Shulsinger Bros., 1952), *Hilhot Isuray Lashon HaRa*, pp. 98–99, *klal* 5, no. 7.
386   *Shulhan Arukh, Hoshen Mishpat* 359:9, 10.
387   Deuteronomy 25:13–15; *Shulhan Arukh, Hoshen Mishpat* 231:3.

Chapter 19   Everyday Ethics

page
391   See Rabbi Aryeh Z. Ginzberg, *Divray Hakhamim* (Brooklyn, NY: Rabbi Z. Berman Books, 1986), p. 236, no. 14.

page

392   See further Rabbi Mosheh Shternbuch, *Teshuvot veHanhagot* (Jerusalem: Netivot HaTorah V'haHesed, 1986), p. 290, no. 829.

393   *Shulhan Arukh, Hoshen Mishpat* 228:6.

394   Deuteronomy 4:15. See also *Gittin* 10b.

395   See *Shulhan Arukh, Hoshen Mishpat* 427:7.

396   Tosefta, *Bava Batra* 1:7.

397   *Mekhilta* to Exodus 23:1.

398   See the forceful argument of Rabbi Yisrael Meir HaKohen, *Sefer Hafetz Hayyim* (New York: Shulsinger Bros., 1952), *Hilkhot Isuray Lashon HaRa*, pp. 39–40, *klal* 1 n. 1 (in *Be'er Mayim Hayyim*).

399   Ibid., *Hilkhot Isuray Lashon HaRa*, p. 142, *klal* 8 n. 10.

400   See Rabbi Samson Raphael Hirsch, *Chapters of the Fathers* (New York: Philipp Feldheim, 1967), p. 10.

401   *Shulhan Arukh, Yoreh De'ah* 249: 1.

402   Rabbenu Yehiel, *Maalot HaMidot* (Jerusalem: Eshkol, 1968), pp. 286–288, under category of *nedivut*.

Glossary

Adonai Lord, referring to God.

Aliyah Call to the Torah.

Amen So be it; the response to a blessing.

Am haaretz Boor, ignoramus.

Amidah Main prayer containing many supplicative blessings.

Aravot Willows, used during Sukkot.

Arbaah Turim Outstanding work of Rabbi Yaakov ben Asher (14th century) that forms the basis for the *Code of Jewish Law*.

Ark Place where Torah scroll is housed.

Aron Kodesh Holy Ark containing Torah scrolls.

Aseh To affirm, as in affirmative commands (*mitzvot aseh*).

Ashkenazi (pl. Ashkenazim) European (mainly German) Jewry and descendants; alternatively, refers to the customs of these people.

Aufruf Call to the Torah prior to a wedding.

Av Name of a month in the Jewish calendar; can also mean "father."

Ayin Name of a letter of the Hebrew alphabet; can also mean "eye."

Aykhah Book of Lamentations, read on Tishah B'Av.

Bar mitzvah Age of responsibility for boys (attained at entry into fourteenth year).

Barukh HaShem L'Olam Prayer recited at the evening (*Maariv*) service just before the *Amidah* (main prayer of nineteen blessings).

Bat mitzvah Age of responsibility for girls (attained at entry into thirteenth year).

Bava Metzia Name of a talmudic tractate.

Bayit House; alternatively, encasement for *tefillin* parchments.

Berakhah Blessing.

Berakhot Plural of *berakhah*, blessings; alternately, name of a talmudic tractate.

Barukh Rofay Holim Blessed be God Who heals the sick.

Bet Din Rabbinic court.

Bet HaMikdash Holy Sanctuary.

Bet Knesset House of Gathering for prayer.

Bimah Center stage.

Birkhat HaGomel Blessing of gratitude for having been saved from peril.

Birkhat HaMazon After-Meal Thanks, popularly referred to as Grace after Meals.

Birkhat Kohanim   Blessing pronounced by *Kohen* (descendant of Aharon the Great *Kohen*) or *kohanim* (pl.) on the people.

Boray pri hagafen   Who creates the fruit of the vine, the blessing recited before drinking wine.

Brit milah   Covenantal circumcision.

Cantor   Specially designated person to lead the congregation in prayer.

Code of Jewish Law   Usually a reference to *Shulhan Arukh*, the main work incorporating the vast expanse of Jewish law.

Dibur   Conversation.

Dreidel   Special top played on Hanukah.

Elul   Name of a month in the Jewish calendar.

Eruv   *Shabbat* enclosure allowing carrying within its borders.

Eruv Tavshilin   Mixture of cooked items, to allow preparing on festival for *Shabbat*.

Etrog   Citron, used on Sukkot.

Even HaEzer   One of the four major sections of the *Code of Jewish Law*, dealing mainly with marriage-related matters.

Fast of Gedalyah   Fast coming right after Rosh HaShanah and commemorating the assassination of the Judean governor Gedalyah, which led to the loss of any semblance of autonomy in the land of Israel.

Fast of the Seventeenth of Tamuz   Fast commemorating the breach in the wall of Jerusalem, which was the harbinger of the destruction of the Holy Sanctuary and the thrusting of Israel into exile.

Get   Jewish bill of divorce.

Gimmel   Name of a letter of the Hebrew alphabet.

Hadassim   Myrtle branches, used on Sukkot.

Haftarah   Prophetic reading that follows Torah reading on *Shabbat* and festival mornings and the afternoon of fasts.

Hagav   A permissible swarmy thing, usually identified as a grasshopper, but whose exact identity is uncertain.

Hagbahah   Lifting the Torah at conclusion of the reading.

Hag Kasher veSameah   Greeting for Passover, meaning "Have a kosher and happy festival."

Hag Sameah   Greeting for any festival, meaning "Have a happy festival."

Hag Urim Sameah   Greeting for Hanukah, meaning "Have a happy Festival of Lights."

Hahodesh   Refers to a special additional biblical reading around the beginning of the month of *Nisan* and dealing with preparations for Passover, which occurs in *Nisan*.

Hakamat Matzayvah Establishing the monument for a deceased person.

Halakhah Jewish law applied to life.

Halakhic Pertaining to the *halakhah*.

Hallah Bread loaf; alternatively, special offering.

Hametz Leavened food products, forbidden on Passover.

Hanukah Eight-day festival of dedication, or lights.

Hanukiah Hanukah *menorah* (candelabra of eight branches).

HaShem The Name, a reference to God.

Hasid Pious person; also refers to disciple of a hasidic master or *rebbe*.

Hatan Groom.

Hatov vehamaytiv Who does good (for me) and makes good (for others), a blessing recited on certain occasions.

Havdalah Ceremony marking the conclusion of *Shabbat* and festivals.

Hazzan Cantor; person designated to lead prayer services.

Heh Name of a letter of the Hebrew alphabet.

Heshvan Name of a month in the Jewish calendar.

Het Name of a letter of the Hebrew alphabet.

Hesped Mournful eulogy.

Hillul HaShem Desecration of God's Name.

Hol Ordinary.

Hol HaMoed Festive period between first and last days of Pesah and Sukkot.

Horayot Name of a talmudic tractate.

Hoshen Mishpat One of the four main sections of the *Code of Jewish Law*, dealing mainly with laws related to money and property.

Hulsha Weakness.

Hupah Canopy under which weddings take place.

Kaddish Sanctification affirmation recited following death of parents and other relatives.

Kaparot Atonement ceremony before Yom Kippur.

Karov Root word meaning "to bring near."

Kashrut Usually pertaining to dietary laws dealing with what may be eaten.

Kedushah Sanctification declaration recited during repeat of the *Amidah*.

Kesef Mishneh Commentary on the *Mishneh Torah* of Maimonides, written by the author of the *Shulhan Arukh*, Rabbi Yosef Karo (16th century).

Ketubah Wedding contract delineating essential marital obligations.

Ketuvot Name of a talmudic tractate.

Khof Name of a letter of the Hebrew alphabet.

Kiddush Sanctification ushering in *Shabbat* or a festival.

Kiddushin Betrothal; alternately, name of talmudic tractate.

Kiddush Levanah Sanctification prayer recited in the presence of the moon in the first half of every month.

Kinot Elegies recited on Tishah B'Av.

Kipah Head covering.

Kittel Special white cloak worn on Yom Kippur, among other occasions.

Kodesh Holy, as in Holy Ark (*Aron Kodesh*).

Kohen (pl. *Kohanim*) Descendant of Aharon, specially designated to serve in and administer the *Bet HaMikdash* and retaining special status today.

Kol Nidray Statement renouncing vows, recited at start of Yom Kippur.

Korban Sacrifice.

Kosher Fit, meeting the legal requirements; usually but not always refers to the permissibility of food.

Kriyah Tearing of garment following loss of any of the seven main relatives.

Kezayit Food the size of an olive.

Lag B'Omer Thirty-third day of the forty-nine-day mourning period between Pesah and Shavuot, a day of celebration.

LeShanah Tovah Literally, for a good year; an erroneous phrase.

LeShanah Tovah Tikatayvi veTayhataymi Greeting to females on Rosh HaShanah, meaning "You should be written and inscribed for a good year."

LeShanah Tovah Tikatayvu veTayhataymu Greeting to males on Rosh HaShanah, meaning "You should be written and inscribed for a good year."

Levite Member of Levitic tribe who ministered in *Bet HaMikdash* and helped the *Kohanim* and who retain special status to this day.

Lo Taaseh Prohibitive commandment; literally, do not.

Lo Tirtzah Do not murder.

Lulav Palm branch, used on Sukkot.

Lug Liquid measurement, about thirteen ounces.

Maariv Evening prayer.

Maftir Concluding Torah reading.

Mamzer Child born as a result of consanguineous or adulterous relationship.

Manot Literally, portions, usually of food.

Marah Place of encampment for Israelites prior to arriving at Mount Sinai.

Maspid Person delivering *hesped*.

Matzah Unleavened bread, the basic staple for Passover.

Mazal Destiny.

Megillat Esther Scroll of Esther, read during Purim services.

Mehitzah Structure separating men's and women's sections in a *Bet Knesset*.

Mem Name of a letter of the Hebrew alphabet.

Menorah Seven-branched candelabra.

Mentsch Authentic, admirable human being.

Messiah Redeemer.

Mezizah Drawing out of blood during covenantal circumcision.

Mezuzah (pl. *mezuzot*) Encasement containing biblical excerpts, including *Shema*, and affixed to doors of Jewish homes and establishments.

Mikvah Special body of water for ritual immersion.

Minhah Afternoon prayer.

Minyan Quorum; alternately, number.

Mishkan Portable sanctuary used by Israelites till *Bet HaMikdash* was built.

Mishlo'ah Manot Sending of foodstuff to others on Purim.

Mishnah Berurah Classic work of Rabbi Yisrael Meir HaKohen on *Orah Hayyim*, one of the four main sections of the *Code of Jewish Law*.

Mishneh Torah Major work of Maimonides (12th century), which extracts from the Talmud its major decisions in all areas affecting life.

Mitzvah (pl. *mitzvot*) Commandment.

Mitzvot aseh Affirmative commandments.

Mitzvot lo taaseh Prohibitive commandments.

Mo'ed Appointed time; also one of six sections of the Mishnah, a component of the Talmud.

Mohel One who performs covenantal circumcisions.

Mosheh Rabbenu Mosheh our master teacher, the one who transmitted the Torah to the people of Israel.

Motzaay Shabbat Saturday night; the conclusion of *Shabbat*.

Mount Sinai Mountain on which the Torah was transmitted.

Musaf Additional prayer for special occasions, usually festivals.

Nes gadol hayah poh A great miracle occurred here.

Nes gadol hayah sham A great miracle occurred there.

Nihum avelim Comforting of mourners.

Nun Name of a letter of the Hebrew alphabet.

Omer Special seven-week period linking Pesah and Shavuot.

Onan Mourner in time period between death and burial.

Oneg Delight.

Orah Hayyim One of the four main sections of the *Code of Jewish Law*, dealing mainly with daily and special-days matters.

Paschal lamb The offering that in Holy Sanctuary times was the main food, together with *matzah*, at the Passover *seder*.

Pelag HaMinhah One-and-a-quarter twelfths of the day prior to sunset, the earliest time after which one may usher in *Shabbat* and recite *Maariv*.

Pesah Passover, Festival of Freedom.

Pidyon Haben Redemption of the firstborn son.

Pirkay Avot *Chapters of the Sages*, a talmudic tractate on ethics.

Purim Feast of Lots.

Rabbenu Gershom Great 11th-century sage who enacted various regulations designed to protect women.

Rabbinic court Court composed of rabbinic scholars to judge cases or to finalize certain procedures, such as divorce or conversion.

Re'ah Neighbor; alternatively, spouse.

Rebbe Rabbinic teacher.

Retzuah (pl. *retzuot*) Leather strap of the *tefillin*.

Revi'it Liquid measurement (about three fluid ounces).

Rosh HaShanah Beginning ("head") of Jewish year.

Rosh Hodesh Beginning ("head") of the month.

Sandek Person holding baby during covenantal circumcision.

Seder Special gathering on Passover evening to relive the Exodus.

Selihot Special prayers of entreaty for pardon.

Sephardi (pl. Sephardim) Descendant of Jews who lived in Spain and Portugal prior to the expulsion in 1492; alternatively, refers to customs of these people.

Seudat Havraah Condolence meal served after funeral.

Shabbat Sabbath (from Friday evening to Saturday night).

Shabbetai Zevi 17th-century false Messiah.

Shabbat Shalom Standard greeting on *Shabbat*, meaning "In the merit of *Shabbat*, you should be blessed with peace."

Shaharit Morning prayer.

Shaliah Tzibbur (abbr. *Shatz*.) Agent of the multitude; cantor.

Shalom Bayit Tranquillity of the home.

Shavuot Festival celebrating receipt of the Torah.

Shehakol nehiyah bidevaro Literally, that all was created by God's word; refers to a blessing for certain types of food and drink.

Sheheheyanu   Blessing of thanks to God (Who has enabled us to reach this moment), recited on special occasions.

Shekel (pl. *shekalim*)   Coin.

Sheloshim   Period of semi-intense mourning following *shivah*, extending to thirty days after the funeral.

Shema   Classic faith affirmation.

Shemini Atzeret   Eighth day of solemn assembly, following seven days of Sukkot.

Shemonah Esray   Also referred to as *Amidah*, main prayer usually containing nineteen blessings.

Sheva Berakhot   Seven blessings recited at the wedding and postwedding meals.

Shin   Name of a letter of the Hebrew alphabet.

Shivah   Seven-day period of intense mourning following death of any of the seven main relatives.

Shlomoh HaMelekh   King Solomon.

Shofar   Ram's horn, sounded on Rosh HaShanah.

Shohet   Person who carefully prepares meat for eating, according to Jewish law.

Shul   Yiddish for synagogue or *Bet Knesset*.

Shulhan Arukh   *Code of Jewish Law.*

Siddur (pl. *siddurim*)   Prayer book.

Sihah   Idle chatter, gossip.

Simhat Torah   Festival day celebrating completion of the Torah reading cycle and its immediate resumption.

Sukkah   Tabernacle, dwelling place during Sukkot.

Sukkot   Festival of Tabernacles.

Tahanun   Special supplication following the *Amidah*.

Tahor   Ritually integrated.

Tallit   Prayer shawl.

Tallit katan   Small *tallit* worn under the shirt.

Talmud   Multivolumed treatise of the rabbinic sages, which interprets the Torah (Bible) and applies Torah and its principles to everyday life.

Talmudic   Pertaining to the Talmud.

Tamay   Ritually removed.

Tamuz   Name of a month in the Jewish calendar.

Teer'a   You shall be in awe of.

Tefillah   Prayer; alternatively, singular of *tefillin*.

Tefillin   Phylacteries (small leather cases containing Torah excerpts).

Tevet   Name of a month in the Jewish calendar.

Tishah B'Av   Day of mourning commemorating destruction of first and second *Bet HaMikdash*.

Tishray   Name of a month in the Jewish calendar.

Torah   Teaching; generally refers to Scripture, Talmud, and commentary thereon.

Tzitzit   Fringes of the *tallit*.

Yahrzeit   Anniversary of Hebrew date of death, commemorated by surviving family.

Yetzer ra   Tendency toward evil.

Yetzer tov   Tendency toward good.

Yizkor   Memorial prayer recited on Yom Kippur and the festivals.

Yom HaAtzmaut   Israel Independence Day.

Yom Kippur   Day of Atonement.

Yom tov   Festival (literally, good or happy day).

Yoreh De'ah   One of the four main sections of the *Code of Jewish Law*, dealing with various matters, including permissibility of food and drink, honoring parents, circumcision, and mourning regulations.

Zekharyah   Biblical prophet.

Zuz (pl. *zuzim*)   Coin.

Bibliography

Adler, Binyamin. *HaNisuin keHilkhatam*. Jerusalem: HaMesorah, 1984.

Aharon of Barcelona. *Sefer HaHinukh*. Israel: Eshkol Press, 1965.

Aviner, Shlomoh. *Am keLavi*. Jerusalem, 1983.

Ayn Yaakov. 4 vols. New York: Pardes, n. d.

Bulka, Reuven P. *Torah Therapy: Reflections on the Weekly Sedra and Special Occasions*. New York: Ktav Publishing House, 1983.

_____ . *Jewish Marriage: A Halakhic Ethic*. Hoboken NJ: Ktav Publishing House; New York: Yeshiva University Press, 1986.

_____ . "Love Your Neighbor: Halachic Parameters." *Journal of Halacha and Contemporary Society* 16 (1988): 44–54.

_____ . *The Jewish Pleasure Principle*. New York: Human Sciences Press, 1989.

_____ . *What You Thought You Knew about Judaism: 341 Common Misconceptions about Jewish Life*. Northvale, NJ: Jason Aronson Inc., 1989.

_____ . "Isaac's Blessing—Who Was Deceived?" *Dor LeDor: Our Biblical Heritage* 17 (1989): 185–189.

_____ . "The Selling of the Birthright: Making Sense of a Perplexing Episode." *The Jewish Bible Quarterly: Dor LeDor* 19 (1990–1991): 100–104.

_____ . *Jewish Divorce Ethics: The Right Way to Say Goodbye*. Ogdensburg, NY: Ivy League Press, 1992.

_____ . *Critical Psychological Issues: Judaic Perspectives*. Lanham, MD: University Press of America, 1992.

Dvorkes, Yeshayahu Aryeh and Yehoshua. *Siddur Minhat Yerushalayim: Kol Bo Hashalem*. Jerusalem, 1977.

Eidlitz, E. *Is It Kosher? Encyclopedia of Kosher Food Facts and Fallacies*. Jerusalem and New York: Feldheim Publishers, 1992.

Eliach, Yaffa. *Hasidic Tales of the Holocaust*. New York: Oxford University Press, 1982.

Encyclopedia Judaica. Jerusalem: Keter Publishing House, 1971.

Epstein, Yehiel Mikhel. *Arukh HaShulhan*. 8 vols. New York: E. Grossman Publishing House, n. d.

Even-Chen, Jacov. *Rabbi Joseph Karo Life Story*. Jerusalem: HaKtav Institute, 1988.

Feinstein, Mosheh. *Igrot Mosheh, Yoreh De'ah 3*. Bnay Brak: Yeshivat Ohel Yosef, 1981.

Felder, A. *Yesodei Smochos.* New York, 1976.

Felder, Gedalyah. *Yesoday Yeshurun.* Vol. 1. New York: J. Biegeleisen, 1977.

———. *Yesoday Yeshurun.* Vol. 6. New York: Balshon, 1970.

———. *Nahalat Zvi.* 2 vols. New York, 1978.

Ganzfried, Shlomoh. *Kitzur Shulhan Arukh.* Tel Aviv: Sinai Publishing, 1974.

Ginzberg, Aryeh. *Divray Hakhamim.* Brooklyn, NY: Rabbi Z. Berman Books, 1986.

Greenwald, Asher Anshil. *Zokher HaBrit.* Israel, 1964.

Greenwald, Meir. *HaSevivon veSevivato: Sefer HaMoadim.* Vol. 5, *Rosh Hodesh, Hanukah, 15th of Shevat.* Tel Aviv: Dvir, 1977.

Greenwald, Yekutiel Yehudah. *Kol Bo al Avelut.* New York: Feldheim, 1965.

Grunfeld, I. *The Jewish Dietary Laws.* 2 vols. London: Soncino Press, 1972.

HaKohen, Yisrael Meir. *Sefer Hafetz Hayyim.* New York: Shulsinger Bros., 1952.

HaLevi, Hayyim David. *Aseh Lekha Rav.* 9 vols. Tel Aviv, 1983.

Henkin, Yosef Eliyahu. *Eydut LeYisrael.* New York: Walden Press, n. d.

Hertz, Joseph. *The Authorized Daily Prayer Book.* New York: Bloch Publishing Company, 1974.

Hirsch, Samson Raphael. *The Pentateuch: Translated and Explained.* 6 vols. London: L. Honig and Sons, 1962.

———. *Chapters of the Fathers.* New York: Philipp Feldheim, 1967.

Jerusalem Talmud. 5 vols. New York: Otzar Hasefarim, 1960.

Landman, Leo, ed. *Judaism and Drugs.* New York: Commission on Synagogue Relations of Federation of Jewish Philanthropies of New York, 1973.

Litvin, Baruch, ed. *The Sanctity of the Synagogue.* New York: Spero Foundation, 1959.

Maimonides, M. *Mishneh Torah.* 6 vols. New York: M. P. Press, 1962.

Meir Simhah of Dvinsk. *Meshekh Hokhmah.* Jerusalem: Eshkol, n. d.

Metzger, Yonah. *MeYam HaHalakhah.* Tel Aviv, 1988.

Mikraot Gedolot. 10 vols. New York: Pardes Publishing House, 1951.

Mishnah Berurah. 6 vols. Jerusalem: Shonah Halakhot, n. d.

Nachshoni, Yehudah. *Hagut BeParshiyot HaTorah.* Bnay Brak, 1979.

Papo, Eliezer. *Pele Yo'etz.* Jerusalem, 1987.

Pelcovitz, Ralph. "Reciting the Hallel on Yom Haatzmaut." *Journal of Halacha and Contemporary Society* 7 (1984): 5–18.

Rabbenu Yehiel. *Maalot HaMidot.* Jerusalem: Eshkol, 1968.

RCA Orthodox Roundtable: Opinion Concerning Metzitzah & AIDS. Available from RCA Roundtable, 5625 Arlington Avenue, Riverdale, NY 10471.

Scherman, Nosson. *The Complete ArtScroll Siddur.* Brooklyn, NY: Mesorah Publications, 1984.

Schwadron, Shalom Mordekhai HaKohen. *Responsa MaHaRSHam.* 4 vols. Jerusalem: Makhon Hatam Sofer, 1974.

Shternbuch, Mosheh. *Responsa Teshuvot veHanhagot.* Jerusalem: Netivot HaTorah V'haHesed, 1986.

Shulhan Arukh. 10 vols. New York: Otzar Halacha, 1965.

Soloff, Emily. "A Muslim Hekhsher." *The Jerusalem Report,* January 17, 1991, pp. 27–29.

Sperling, Abraham. *Taamay HaMinhagim uMekoray HaDinim.* Jerusalem: Eshkol, n. d.

Tal, Shlomoh, ed. *Siddur Rinat Yisrael.* Jerusalem: Morashah Publishing, 1977.

The Holy Scriptures. 2 vols. Philadelphia: Jewish Publication Society, 1965.

The Talmud. Ed. I. Epstein. 18 vols. London: Soncino Press, 1961.

The Talmud. 20 vols. New York: Otzar Hasefarim, 1965.

Tukacinsky, Yehiel Mikhel. *Gesher HaHayyim.* 2 vols. Jerusalem: Solomon Press, 1960.

Wagschal, S. *Torah Guide for the Businessman.* Jerusalem: Feldheim, 1990.

Weiss, Abner. *Death and Bereavement: A Halakhic Guide.* Hoboken, NJ: Ktav Publishing House; New York: Union of Orthodox Jewish Congregations of America, 1991.

Weissberg, Yosef David. *Sefer Otzar HaBrit.* 2 vols. Jerusalem: Machon Torat HaBrit, 1986.

Yosef, Ovadyah. *Yehaveh Daat.* 6 vols. Jerusalem: A. B. Printing, 1977.

Zevin, Shlomoh. *HaMoadim beHalakhah.* Tel Aviv: A Zioni, 1959.

Zucker, Dovid, and Moshe Francis. *Chol HaMoed: Comprehensive Review of the Laws of the Intermediate Days of the Festivals.* Lakewood, NJ: Halacha Publications, 1981.

Index

About the Author

Reuven P. Bulka, rabbi of Congregation Machzikei Hadas in Ottawa, Canada, is a highly regarded author and editor. He was ordained at the Rabbi Jacob Joseph Rabbinical Seminary in 1965 and received his Ph.D. in Logotherapy from the University of Ottawa in 1971. Founder of the Center for the Study of Psychology and Judaism and editor of the *Journal of Psychology and Judaism*, Rabbi Dr. Bulka is the author of twenty-five books, including *What You Thought You Knew about Judaism*, and scores of articles.